"*Regardless of the crisis you are facing, you* testimony. God can move any mountain. problem."

Dr. Brian Disney, Senior Pastor
Mission Boulevard Baptist Church, Fayetteville, Arkansas

"*Sometimes God's answers to your prayers will surprise you. Dr. Briney never expected the answer to his prayer to be life threatening. But the Lord granted his prayer with a healing miracle.*"

Jerry Locke, Retired Pastor and Author
Lakeworth, Texas

"*Pat was an incredible fighter during his illness. Although he fought through two bouts of Hodgkin's lymphoma, he never lost hope and never stopped praying! His battle with cancer didn't quench his desire to know God in a more intimate way. This book reveals how the impossible becomes possible through prayer!*"

Lepaine Sharp-McHenry, DNP, RN
Dean and Professor, College of Natural, Behavioral, and Health Sciences, Simmons University

"*Some things cannot be fixed but by prayer and a miracle. Dr. Briney's testimony will inspire you to pray and expect a miracle.*"

P.D. Taylor, Pastor
Pleasant Valley Baptist Church, Dallas, Texas

"*Dr. Briney's two books, HOPE and PRAY, will inspire you to pray. If you feel discouraged about your prayer life, these books will give you hope to pray and wisdom to pray more effectively. You will not be disappointed.*"

Doug Hammett, Author and Missionary
South Africa

PRAY

HOW GOD ANSWERS EVERY PRAYER

DR. PATRICK BRINEY

PRAY: How God Answers Every Prayer
© 2020 Patrick Briney

For information, please write:

> Permissions Coordinator, Life Changing Scriptures
> 2006 Mission Boulevard, Fayetteville, Arkansas 72703
> www.lifechangingscriptures.org/permission

Books may be purchased from Life Changing Scriptures for educational, business, or sales promotional uses. For information on quantity purchases, please write:

> Educational Purchases, Life Changing Scriptures
> 2006 Mission Boulevard, Fayetteville, Arkansas 72703
> www.lifechangingscriptures.org/bulk-purchases

Book 1 in this series: HOPE: Lessons from a Cancer Survivor's Journey with God / Patrick Briney

Book 2 in this series: PRAY: How God Answers Every Prayer / Patrick Briney

1. Religion 2. Christian 3. Prayer. I. Title.

ISBN: 978-1-951169-01-5

Scripture quotations are from the King James Version of the Bible.

Cover design and interior layout by Exodus Design Studio.

CONTENTS

PREFACE

In 1989, I was diagnosed with stage 4 Hodgkin's lymphoma, and five years later it reoccurred. That was over thirty years ago. This is my story of what God taught me about prayer through the experience of having cancer.

A year prior to being diagnosed with cancer, I had asked the Lord to teach me about the prayers that move mountains. He taught me by giving me a mountain. I prayed, and God moved it.

More importantly, I gained some great insights into prayer. My first book, *HOPE: Lessons from a Cancer Survivor's Journey with God*, explains why God healed me. This second book explains many of the lessons I learned about prayer.

One person's journey involves others. Many people have shared my experiences. I am grateful to each one including my wife and family, Mom and Dad, brother and sister, their families, my church family, and many friends.

This book was written for the purpose of ministry. I am grateful to our core team Patty Minor, Mary Saldivar, Adriel Wiggins, and Pablo and Lisa Pagliani for sharing this ministry with me. We all hope and pray that you too will discover the love of God in your life and personally experience His power to move mountains.

Pat

INTRODUCTION

If you understand prayer, you will always have hope.

In high school, I had a 1951 Ford pickup. I painted it school bus yellow. The trim and tire rims were shiny black. It was beautiful. I added an eight-track player and oogah horn. It was perfect. But it wasn't all for show. It was a work truck. I used it to carry

Prayer does not change God. Prayer changes people and circumstances.

real estate signs every weekend for new housing development announcements and to haul things to the swap meet every Saturday. I was a sign "bootlegger" for local real estate companies, and I was the guy they called to declutter houses abandoned by renters. The truck was perfect, and I took care of it to keep it in good shape.

But throwing signs in and out of the truck and loading and unloading furniture and bulky items inevitably resulted in scratches and smudges on the truck. I had to constantly care for the truck and fix weekly damage. It was a cycle of perfection and imperfection. So why am I telling you this?

We live in a world of decay and imperfection. And the changes we need are far more significant than scratches on a truck. Prayer changes things that we cannot change ourselves.

Prayer does not change God. Prayer changes people and circumstances. God does not need to change. We need to change. God is perfect. We are imperfect.

Ok, at this point some are already asking, "How can a perfect God create something imperfect like us?" The answer is simple. He doesn't. There is a difference between creating something perfect and creating something permanently perfect. Confusing perfection with permanence leads to a wrong conclusion. God created man perfect. Man chose to be imperfect. I am talking about Adam and Eve. They represent the rest of us.

My truck was "perfect" at the beginning of the week after I cleaned it, but by the end of the week, it was imperfect. Similarly, God created Adam and Eve perfect in every way. He did not make them permanently perfect. God gave them the choice to continue in perfection. All they had to do was to heed His warnings about how to avoid imperfection.

I learned that heeding warning labels on machines, cars, and appliances is important. If you try to use a machine to do things it was not designed for, you will break the machine. If you put water in the gas tank of a car, it will stop running. This is not a problem with the design of the machine. It is a problem with the user failing to follow the instructions and to heed the warnings of the maker.

In college, I took a computer programming class. One day we were coding in the lab, and a student was complaining about the need to use a semicolon at the end of a line of code. She could not understand why the computer would not run her program. She called it a dumb machine. All she lacked was a semicolon. The teacher told her computers are dumb machines. They only do what they are designed to do. Respect the design, and the machine will work.

And so it is with us. God designed us perfectly, but when we do not heed His warning, we violate His design. This is called sin. When we sin, we break down and break things around us. Sin ruins our prayer life. Worst of all, we die. Sin is fatal.

PRAY!

In my book *HOPE: Lessons from a Cancer Survivor's Journey with God*, I share that God gave me a mountain that could not be moved without Him.

He was the only one who could change my circumstances and health. He is the only one who could preserve my life for thirty years after stage 4 Hodgkin's lymphoma, its reoccurrence, and the caustic chemotherapy.

God gave me a mountain. He was the only one who could move it.

My second bout with Hodgkin's lymphoma was not a surprise. I had been treated for stage 4 Hodgkin's lymphoma. The odds were against my five-year survival. Sure enough, five years later, it came back. At the time, there were not enough five-year survivors with reoccurring lymphoma to calculate a statistically valid survival rate. My doctor said that he had not successfully treated anyone in my condition. My bout with cancer was my mountain. It occurred the year I asked God to teach me about prayers that move mountains. I was diagnosed with cancer the week I completed my study on prayer.

I shared in my first book how God answered my prayer to understand prayers that move mountains, not only through His Word, but through experience. *HOPE: Lessons from a Cancer Survivor's Journey with God* was written to give hope and inspiration for those wanting to learn what prayer can do. God healed me. He moved my mountain.

In this book, I show how you can have every prayer granted. I explain how God always answers each of the four types of prayer, and I describe the amazing benefits of intercessory prayer. These are exciting lessons that you can apply and share with others.

Learning by experience personalizes the insights gained and develops deeper convictions. When you learn by experience, lessons become a part of your life for the rest of your life. Experiences change you. I was changed by my bout with cancer and by my experience with prayer.

I don't just *talk* about prayer. I share my *experience* with prayer. I am humbled to share such experiences. I do not claim to know all about prayer. I am still learning, and I share what I have learned thus far.

Prayer is a conversation with God, and conversation requires a relationship. My relationship with God began when I trusted Jesus Christ as my Savior in February of 1977. I trusted Him with my life. I believed in Him and in His teachings. I wanted His will and plan for my life. I trusted Him to guide me through life. To this day I continue to pray, "Lord, live your life through me. I am your willing vessel. Do as you please with my life. I confess that I am the weak link in understanding and application. But I am willing to do my best."

I am happy to share with you that experiencing a relationship with God is real, and God has used my testimony to encourage and teach others to live for Christ and to pray better.

Why do I seek to understand prayer? I have this nagging

curiosity to understand. I want to experience my relationship with God. I want to experience prayers that move mountains. I want to avoid doing things that would prevent me from experiencing these things. So I am compelled to surrender to Him with anticipation of His will for my life. I don't want to miss out on anything. I don't want to find out in heaven what could have been if only I had surrendered to Him.

The thoughts and lessons in this book come from my personal experience. After a year of focused study about prayer and reading and thinking about every verse I could find in the Bible about prayer, the Lord put me through the school of experience to teach me more about prayer. He answered my prayers to understand prayer by including application and experience.

I think you will enjoy the lessons I have learned just as others have. These lessons are exciting. I had one high school student tell me that the lessons made him want to pray more. My prayer is that you too will want to pray more and that you will experience the granting of your prayers.

OUTLINE TO UNDERSTANDING PRAYER

The purpose of prayer is Communion, Praise, and Requests (CPR).

Four foundational truths of prayer

1. God is in control at all times.
2. God hears every prayer.
3. God answers every prayer.
4. God's answers are always the best answers.

Criteria for prayers to be granted

- God's will for saving the maximum number of souls

- Minimum requirements: faith, belief, righteousness
- Extra mile prayers: persistence and fasting

The four types of prayer

1. Prayers for revelation
2. Prayers for desires
3. Prayers because of revelation
4. Prayers because God answers

Answers to prayers

1. God answers every prayer.
2. Some answers are a definite yes or no.
3. Some answers are silent, leaving the choice up to you.
4. Some answers are silent, requiring that you wait on God.

Intentional prayer requirements

1. Time
2. Subject
3. Focus

1
PRAYING FOR REVELATION

Blessed is the man that trusteth in the LORD,
and whose hope the LORD is.
—Jeremiah 17:7

Why did I have cancer? Was I being judged and chastised? Did I do something wrong? Was this a random disease that could happen to anyone? Was this an answer to my prayers to learn about prayer?

After receiving the news about having cancer, I spent two weeks in prayer asking God to reveal to me what He wanted me to pray for. I needed to know how to think correctly about the outcome. What did He have planned for me? Should I pray for healing? Should I pray for a comfortable death? Was there a good reason for God to keep me around?

GOD'S WILL

After being told that I had cancer, I wondered whether I should pray for my life. I asked the Lord, "Is this Your will? How can I know your will? How can I know that this prayer is worth praying? Why is it so hard to know what to pray? What am I doing wrong? What am I not understanding?" I just wanted to know what the right prayer was for me.

Isaiah 1:18 invites, "Come now, and let us reason together, saith the LORD: though your sins be as scarlet, they shall be as white as snow; though they be red like crimson, they shall be as wool." God created us to be intelligent and reasonable. So I have the perspective that God is one to be reasoned with. He has answers and explanations for our questions. We may not always like the answers, but I believe that, since they come from God, they are always the best answers.

In Isaiah 41:20–21, God explains that He does things "That they may see, and know, and consider, and understand together, that the hand of the LORD hath done this, and the Holy One of Israel hath created it. Produce your cause, saith the LORD; bring forth your strong reasons, saith the King of Jacob." God wants us to understand Him and to reason with Him.

God wants us to understand Him and to reason with Him.

Obviously, we cannot know the infinite mind of God, but we can learn and know what is important. We have the ability to discover, to learn, and to apply knowledge. Though there is vastly more to learn about Earth, the oceans, and space, we nonetheless have learned enough to make life more comfortable than it was a hundred years ago. With every discovery, we are amazed at the new applications that are possible. So then, although we can never know very much about an infinite God, we can still know enough about Him to make important decisions. God wants us to understand Him. He wants us to understand the world we live in. He wants us to present our reasons to Him and to compare notes. He made us this way. He made us to be intelligent and thoughtful, to ask Him questions, and to learn.

Because of this perspective, I ask God about things. I ask for understanding about how and why He does things. I am not challenging or questioning what He does. I do not question His motives. I ask to understand. I like to make sense out of the world I live in. Who better to seek answers from than God? I find it ironic that I asked God to teach me more about Him and prayers to move mountains, and the answer from Him required me to understand more about myself.

NOT AFRAID OF GOD

I prayed to understand the prayers that move mountains, and God taught me through the experience of facing death by cancer. Did I pray for cancer? No. I don't know anyone in their right mind who would pray to have cancer or any other crisis. Should I have been more cautious in my prayer? I am amazed that, when I share my testimony with others, many caution me to be careful about what I pray for. Apparently, some think that praying for God's will to be done or asking God to teach them something should be done cautiously. They fear what God might do to them or require of them. But this means *they* are fearful of God and of His plan for their lives. And they are cautioning others to be fearful of God and not to seek God's plan.

I remember when I was a kid hearing someone at school talk about being a missionary and the problems they encountered. I didn't want that to happen to me. It made me afraid to ask God what His plan was for my life. I think it is normal for people to think this way. They can't imagine intentionally putting themselves in harm's way. They hear stories about the hardships

3

of others that are attributed to God, and they fear asking for God's will to be done in their lives.

But praying for God's will to be done in your life is not about praying for problems or trials. It is about praying to make your life meaningful, to make it count for something. It is about experiencing the best possible plan for your life, God's plan. If anything should be feared, it is *not* knowing and doing God's will.

First Corinthians 10:13 assures us with an important promise, saying, "There hath no temptation taken you but such as is common to man: but God [is] faithful, who will not suffer you to be tempted above that ye are able; but will with the temptation also make a way to escape, that ye may be able to bear [it]." What God calls us to do, He equips us to do. Different people are equipped to fulfill different purposes. You do not have to worry about what others do for God. Just focus on what God wants you to do. He will equip you as needed.

I know that God can always be trusted. *You* can trust Him too. You can trust Him to save you. You can trust Him to fulfill His promise of grace. You can trust Him to do what is best for you. You can trust Him no matter what happens to you in this life.

I did not pray for cancer. I did not pray for suffering. I prayed for His will to be done. It was done, and it was rewarding in more ways than I am aware of. The presence of God during my illness was an amazing experience. The answers to prayers were reassuring. The insights given were very rewarding. The expanded ministry was fulfilling.

Let me assure you that I pray to be delivered from evil and not to be led into temptations. I pray that His will be done. I am not afraid of God, and I want to experience His blessings to the fullest extent. I do not want to hold back. I do not want to limit God. I want only to give Him my all, which means primarily trying to stay out of His way and not to interfere with His plan.

Everyone should trust God and pray to know and to do His will. There is no better way to live than God's way. You can't go wrong. You can only experience the best plan for your life.

SUFFERING

When we choose to sin, we condone the sins of all others. We may not approve of the sins others choose, but just as we are given the opportunity to choose our preferred sins, others are given the same opportunity. So when we choose our favorite sins, we condone the choice to commit all sins. We live in a world that we helped build.

> When we choose our favorite sins, we condone the choice to commit all sins. We live in a world that we helped build.

Not convinced? Let's look at it from God's perspective, rather than ours. All sins are choices to rebel against God. Regardless of the sin, the *choice* to sin is an act of disobedience. All sins are rebellion against God's will. One choice to rebel against an infinite God is the same as any other choice to rebel.

All sins begin with the same sin of choosing to disobey God. Once the choice to rebel is made, we enter into the world of lawlessness to choose any other sin. This means that, regardless of the differences between sins, they all begin the same way, namely, with a decision to disregard God's will.

If you choose to disregard God's will, then you implicitly condone everyone's right to disregard God's will. The choice of sins after this point is secondary. When you make the choice to sin, you condone the lawless choices of others, regardless of their preferred sins. It would be hypocritical to choose the sin of your preference and then deny others the sins of their preference. I am not saying this makes sin right. God determines what is right.

Are some sins worse than others? Yes. God makes this clear in the Law He gave to Israel with the saying "eye for eye and tooth for tooth." *Among us*, different sins deserve different consequences. But *with God*, all sins are infinitely offensive. Therefore, all sins are equally condemned in His eyes.

> With God, all sins are infinitely offensive. Therefore, all sins are equally condemned in His eyes.

We live in a lawless world of rebellion with other rebels. We know there is a Law, and we try to make our own laws for the sake of security and order. But when we pick and choose the laws we will obey, we live in a lawless culture. And the more people there are who choose to live without regard for laws, the more lawless we become.

We all rebel against God's will, and therefore, we all contribute to the way the world is now. No one is traveling down God's perfect path of peace and well-being. At best, some are *trying* to travel the best path. Fortunately, the day is coming when all believers who call out to Jesus Christ for mercy and grace will have the opportunity to begin again in a perfect world with perfect bodies in the new heaven and earth promised in Revelation 21–22.

Living in a world of rebellion means there may be nothing you can do about the choices of others. Unless you are bigger and stronger in some way and can protect yourself, living with rebels is dangerous. This is not to say that there are not people who understand the value of law and order or that no one wants to live in peace. Humanity was designed for these things. This is God's perfect plan. But in a world of rebellion, things only get worse, not better. This is the reason that God judged the earth with a flood. Genesis 6:5 says, "And GOD saw that the wickedness of man was great in the earth, and that every imagination of the thoughts of his heart was only evil continually." After Noah and his family, humanity went down the same path as their forefathers prior to the flood, and God scattered them from the tower of Babel. The Apostle Paul said in Second Timothy 3:13, "But evil men and seducers shall wax worse and worse, deceiving, and being deceived." Sadly, the victims that evil seeks include the ones who seek to be helpful, rather than to do harm. Second Timothy 3:12 says, "Yea, and all that will live godly in Christ Jesus shall suffer persecution." Living in a world of rebellion means living in a world of suffering.

It is important to remember that every time you choose to sin, you condone this kind of world. When I say you condone sin, I am not saying sin is justified. Sin is always wrong and always brings suffering. And I am not saying that you like the end result. God has warned from the beginning that there are consequences to sin. I am saying that, when you sin, you share in the responsibility for the suffering in the world.

When you sin, you share in the responsibility for the suffering in the world.

Suffering is a part of living in a world of sin that you help to make. And unfortunately, you may end up hurt because of the choices others make. Some people delight in hurting others. They have no regard for God, for laws, or for others. These are the choices they make. But their choices to sin, whether they affect you personally or not, do not dictate your choices. You can always make the right choices, regardless of the choices others make. You can always choose to do right, to live for God, and to glorify Him with your testimony. Paul wrote in Second Timothy 3:14, after saying that the days will get more evil, "But continue thou in the things which thou hast learned and hast been assured of, knowing of whom thou hast learned them."

Some people question God's motives and even His existence because of their personal suffering. But God's worthiness is not determined by His deliverance of believers from harm in this world of sin. He is holy and perfect because of who He is. He is worthy to be honored because He is God, not because of what happens to you.

He endured much more suffering than any other human. Even the most horrendous circumstances experienced among humans are infinitesimally smaller than God's sufferings. He sympathizes. He understands pain and sorrow. He understands injustice. He is our God, who knows our sorrows and has experienced our infirmities. Hebrews 4:15 says, "For we have not an high priest which cannot be touched with the feeling of our infirmities; but was in all points tempted like as we are, yet without sin."

I am amazed by the story of Job's suffering in the Bible. He was a man who understood God's worthiness. Even after he suffered the devastating loss of his children, possessions, property, and friends, he said in Job 1:21–22, "…Naked came I out of my mother's womb, and naked shall I return thither: the LORD gave, and the LORD hath taken away; blessed be the name of the LORD. In all this Job sinned not, nor charged God foolishly."

God does not have to prove Himself to us. His greatness, His compassion, and His power remain the same, whether we suffer or not, and whether we believe Him or not. God is worthy because of who He is, not because someone approves of what He does. We all answer to God as our Creator. He answers to no one. He has no need to prove Himself to anyone.

The world of sorrow and pain we live in is the result of our doing what God told us *not* to do. We tell God to leave us alone so that we can do as we please. How then can we justify our complaint that He does not care when He is granting our request and leaving us to fend for ourselves?

The day is coming when God will establish His kingdom on Earth, and it will be free of sin, suffering, and death. He will show us how it could have been if we had listened to Him. In the meantime, we must endure the sorrows that come with being in a world of sin.

Nonetheless, God does help. As stated above, First Corinthians 10:13 says, "There hath no temptation taken you but such as is common to man: but God [is] faithful, who will not suffer you to be tempted above that ye are able; but will with the temptation also make a way to escape, that ye may be able to bear [it]." In some cases, God delivers people *from* tragedy. In other cases, He delivers them *through* tragedy.

In some cases, God delivers people from tragedy. In other cases, He delivers them through tragedy.

Sometimes in tragedy, God gives comfort and peace to endure the suffering. Philippians 4:7 says, "And the peace of God, which passeth all understanding, shall keep your hearts and minds through Christ Jesus." Other times, God removes the suffering while in a tragedy.

Regardless of how God chooses to deliver you, pray for comfort. Pray for strength. Pray that God's will be done. And pray that you will remain faithful to Him, regardless of your circumstances.

SUFFERING WAS NOT MY PRAYER

I do not want to suffer. No one does. I think it is a terrible tragedy that anyone has to suffer. But suffering is a fact of life, from natural disasters to vicious attacks by evil people.

Is suffering the result of failing to pray enough? Is it God's desire that we suffer? Is it possible to eliminate all suffering with prayers? No. No. No. The choice to sin and to do things our own way causes suffering. From the beginning, God has desired that no one sin and suffer. Inevitably, everyone sins, everyone suffers, and everyone dies. There is no escape from suffering in a sin-filled world. God warned us of the consequences. Now He offers help along the paths of our lives.

Suffering in this world cannot be avoided. And if God's plan for my life includes suffering so that I can be taught or improve my ministry to others, then let it be. But if it can be avoided, by all means let it be avoided; nevertheless, not my will, but God's be done.

It cannot be said often enough in our culture of complaint and selfishness that God does not want us to suffer. In Luke 11:4, Jesus told His disciples to pray, "… lead us not into temptation; but deliver us from evil." This is a prayer recommended by Christ. Sometimes, this prayer is granted immediately. Other times, it is postponed. But for all believers, it will be granted after departing this world of sin. Revelation 7:16–17 describes the ending that all believers look forward to. "They shall hunger no more, neither thirst any more; neither shall the sun light on them, nor any heat. For the Lamb which is in the midst of the throne shall feed them, and shall lead them unto living fountains of waters: and God shall wipe away all tears from their eyes."

God does not want people to experience pain and misery. Revelation 21:4 shows us that His plan is to establish a pain-free future for us. "And God shall wipe away all tears from their eyes; and there shall be no more death, neither sorrow, nor crying, neither shall there be any more pain: for the former things are passed away." Since the beginning, God has wanted to bless humanity with paradise. It all began in the Garden of Eden. Every need was taken care of. But we, like Adam and Eve, have chosen sin and its consequences, rather than God and His blessings. We are living in a world of our own making. We have told Him to leave us alone and to let us do our own thing. *We* have made this world a place of suffering.

Jesus' words to Israel in the days leading up to His crucifixion describe very well how we created our problem. In Matthew 23:37, Jesus says, "O Jerusalem, Jerusalem, thou that killest the prophets, and stonest them which are sent unto thee, how often would I have gathered thy children together, even as a hen gathereth her chickens under her wings, and ye would not!" Sin makes life tough, but it was our choice to do things our way rather than God's way. Now we know God was right. And until He restores things back to the way they were at the beginning, we must do the best we can in a sin-corrupted world.

> *Sin makes life tough, but it was our choice to do things our way rather than God's way.*

PRAYER FOR UNDERSTANDING

I did a lot of soul searching for several weeks after being told I had cancer. I was trying to sort out my feelings, to think about getting my house in order, and to understand what God was doing in my life. How should I pray? Should I pray for healing? Should I ask for nothing and let the cancer take its course? Was God punishing me? Was I being punished for the sins of others in the church (like the sin of Achan in the Old Testament)? Was God answering a prayer of mine to take my life if that would be beneficial for saving the souls of others? Was my cancer just a normal human event, meaning I was a statistic?

My only desire was that God's will be done. I found myself unable to pray for healing or deliverance for two weeks after being told I had cancer. I did not have direction from the Lord to pray one way or another. To pray for healing seemed selfish.

Many people die from disease, even good Christian men, women, and children. Why should I ask for special treatment? I could not pray for myself.

One night I read a fictional story about a Christian, pioneer family traveling westward. The theme of hope and strength in hard times impressed me. I reflected on my own difficulty and felt relieved that God was going to see me through my cancer. Furthermore, I was being selfish by not praying for God's healing in my life.

Four months before I was diagnosed with cancer, our first baby, Lisa, was born. I wanted to be a part of her life. And I thought how important it was for a little girl to have in her life a daddy who loves her. Lisa was worth praying for. I could pray for my healing because of her. And there was Colleen. I knew that Colleen could be self-sufficient if she needed to be. But we had pledged our lives to each other, and I was responsible to do all that I could to be with her. Immediately, I prayed for all of us.

Also, there is much to do in ministry until the Lord returns. There is a spiritual warfare for the salvation of souls. I want to be a part of fighting for truth in that warfare. It seems that there are such great needs on mission fields and so few laborers. I thought of Christ's words when He said, "Then saith he unto his disciples, The harvest truly is plenteous, but the labourers are few; Pray ye therefore the Lord of the harvest, that he will send forth labourers into his harvest" (Matthew 9:37–38). And the words of Isaiah 6:8 kept repeating in my mind. It says, "… I heard the voice of the Lord, saying, Whom shall I send, and who will go for us? Then said I, Here am I; send me." I immediately prayed for souls and my participation in ministry.

And then there was the context of my year long prayer and study. I had been praying to understand and experience the prayers that move mountains described by Jesus in Mark

11:22—24. "And Jesus answering saith unto them, Have faith in God. For verily I say unto you, That whosoever shall say unto this mountain, Be thou removed, and be thou cast into the sea; and shall not doubt in his heart, but shall believe that those things which he saith shall come to pass; he shall have whatsoever he saith. Therefore I say unto you, What things soever ye desire, when ye pray, believe that ye receive them, and ye shall have them." My study about prayer was only the beginning of the lesson Christ had planned for me. God was taking me the next step into understanding the prayers that move mountains. This was not a study to talk about. It was a lesson to live.

I had asked God what to pray for, and I had my answer. The quiet voice of God was at the forefront of my thoughts. It was undeniable. I knew that God was telling me to pray for my life. There was no doubt in my mind. This was my mountain to move. I was liberated from the hesitancy of doubt and uncertainty, and I prayed with the full confidence that God had told me how to pray.

I was ready to fight this cancer, to be a daddy to my little girl, to be a husband to my wife, to continue as an energetic participant in serving Christ, and to pray prayers that move mountains. I prayed fervently, and I prayed confidently.

During my prayers at that time, James 5:13—15 came to mind, which says, "Is any among you afflicted? let him pray. Is any merry? let him sing psalms. Is any sick among you? let him call for the elders of the church; and let them pray over him, anointing him with oil in the name of the Lord: And the prayer of faith shall save the sick, and the Lord shall raise him up; and if he have committed sins, they shall be forgiven him." According to this verse, I understood that I should ask the elders of the church to pray for me. They did, and they poured oil on my head as they prayed.

COUNTERFEIT REVELATION

The uncertainty I had before and up to the point of knowing how to pray vanished when God granted my prayer to know how to pray. But how could I be sure it was God's voice and not my own thoughts?

> Distinguishing God's revelation from self-revelation is possible.

Hebrews 5:14 explains that distinguishing God's revelation from self-revelation is possible. It says, "But strong meat belongeth to them that are of full age, [even] those who by reason of use have their senses exercised to discern both good and evil." Through the exercise of experience and study of God's Word, it is possible to distinguish His voice. For me, the knowledge of what to pray for was very definite and conclusive.

You may not be able to distinguish God's voice, but that does not mean others cannot. Be assured that God wants you to recognize His voice too. Just humble yourself and ask Him to teach you to recognize His voice.

Understandably, those without the experience of faith may be skeptical. But faith is personal revelation from God. It is not given for the purpose of proving God's message to others. It is given to personalize His message to each of us individually. It is not something people can use to demonstrate their power of influence over God like one might use a Genie in a lamp. Faith is from God. It comes on His terms by His will, not by the will of men.

I do not feel the need to prove my faith to anyone, especially an arrogant skeptic. I have heard skeptics taunt God and tempt Him to prove Himself by miraculous events. But I am convinced from experience that most skeptics would remain skeptics even if they saw a miracle. Those who insist on believing that life and our complex and fine-tuned universe exist by some unknown, natural processes in contradiction to known scientific laws will reject other miracles too. They are not interested in finding God. They are only looking for more excuses to dismiss Him.

The uncertainty of being able to recognize the quiet voice of God produces so much anxiety in some that they are prevented from making decisions. This is not how God wants us to live. So what can be done? How do you differentiate God's revelation from counterfeit revelation?

First Corinthians 10:33 is a great beginning point to break out of your doubt. Adopt this attitude: "Whether therefore ye eat, or drink, or whatsoever ye do, do all to the glory of God." Learn about God and His will by studying His Word. If you do your part to devote your life to God, and trust Him, then He will do His part to guide you.

THREE RESOURCES TO DISCERN GOD'S WILL

God has given us three resources to help us discern His will. These are essential for knowing how to pray. The first resource is the *Word of God*. The second is the *Spirit of God*. The third is the *church of God*.

First, study the Word of God to exercise your senses of discernment mentioned in Hebrews 5:12–14. This is the admonition found in Second Timothy 2:15, which says, "Study to shew thyself approved unto God, a workman that needeth not to be ashamed, rightly dividing the word of truth."

Second, rely on the Holy Spirit to guide you. How do you do that? Ephesians 5:18 says, "And be not drunk with wine, wherein is excess; but be filled with the Spirit." To be drunk means to be under the influence of alcohol. This is a conscious choice some make. But the Bible says to put yourself under the controlling influence of the Spirit of God. This is done by consciously yielding yourself to the Holy Spirit. Ask the Holy Spirit to guide you and to help you make the right decisions. Ask Him to show God's will to you as needed. Commit to serving Him and doing His will.

Third, God expects every Christian to be in a local, New Testament church. Ephesians 4:11–12 tells us, "And he gave some, apostles; and some, prophets; and some, evangelists; and some, pastors and teachers; For the perfecting of the saints, for the work of the ministry, for the edifying of the body of Christ." Verse 14 adds, "That we henceforth be no more children, tossed to and fro, and carried about with every wind of doctrine, by the sleight of men, and cunning craftiness, whereby they lie in wait to deceive."

God directs every believer committed to Him to a local church home. Every believer in the book of Acts was baptized and became a member of a local church home. Peter *commanded* some to be baptized (Acts 10:48). Christ's great commission to His disciples included church baptism and participation. In Matthew 28:19, He says, "Go ye therefore, and teach all nations, baptizing them in the name of the Father, and of the Son, and of the Holy Ghost."

Those who want to do God's work God's way ask Him which church He wants them to participate in. God has a plan for all believers to participate in His work of ministry through a local church. He has a local church home for each believer for the purpose of training, protection, and opportunities to serve Him. He gives church leaders the responsibility to train their congregations. The *perfection* mentioned in this verse does not mean to make church members flawless. Only God can do that. It means to help us become spiritually mature.

Together, these three resources help you find and fulfill God's plan for your life. When you read the Word of God, you discover what God wants you to do. The Holy Spirit confirms the Word in your heart by faith, and the elders in your church help you understand its application.

Why study the Word of God, yield to the Spirit of God, and participate in a local, New Testament church? Those having faith understand that this is what God wants them to do. This is what faith is all about. It is about knowing and understanding. This does not mean you will believe it, though you should. By faith, God shows us that we should believe Him and obey Him.

PRAYERS FOR DISCERNMENT

Are you wondering what to pray for? Are you wondering what God's will is for your life? You will be happy to know that discovering God's will is as easy as reading the Bible. So much of God's will is written down in the Bible that anyone who truly wants to know God's will can do so just from reading the Bible. There is absolutely no excuse for not knowing God's will and doing it.

The Bible is the most important source for knowing God's will because it is the obvious, revealed will of God. It is written down so that there is no mistaking what His will is. Everybody can read the Bible and determine God's will. In the Bible, God reveals His will for married men, married women, singles, children, the elderly, believers, and unbelievers. If you are serious about knowing God's will, it is easy to find.

But what about knowing God's will for things that are *not* written in the Bible? What about *your* job, whether *you* should go to college, whom *you* should marry, whether *you* should buy or rent a house, which church ministry *you* should be involved in, whether to home school or not home school, etc.? What is God's will for your life in particular?

Here is the secret to knowing God's unwritten will: be seeking and doing God's written will. If you are not reading your Bible and doing the obvious, then it should not surprise you that God is

The secret to knowing God's unwritten will is to seek and do God's written will. not revealing any more of His will to you. The point is this: if you are unwilling to do the most obvious, then do not plan on knowing the obscure. Either God will not reveal it to you, or you will be too immature to recognize it anyway.

If you are not doing God's written will, you are not capable of recognizing God's unwritten will. If you are doing your own thing, and you are refusing to seek and obey God's written will, how then can you expect to be mature enough to recognize God's will expressed as a quiet voice in your mind?

Most people are looking for the big neon sign proclaiming God's unwritten will for them. But it is not revealed this way. It is not in signs and wonders. It is revealed in His written Word for all eyes to see and by faith in our minds to know.

God's quiet voice is in our minds; it is not heard by others. So how then do we distinguish it from other thoughts in our mind? I am talking about when you think to yourself and have those conversations about what to do. How do you recognize God's voice from your own?

The answer is found in Hebrews 5:11–14, which is a scolding of believers because they were "… dull of hearing. For when for the time ye ought to be teachers, ye have need that one teach you again which be the first principles of the oracles of God; and are become such as have need of milk, and not of strong meat. For every one that useth milk is unskilful in the word of righteousness: for he is a babe. But strong meat belongeth to them that are of full age, even those who by reason of use have their senses exercised to discern both good and evil."

As I mentioned before, recognizing the voice of God requires maturity and the exercise of your senses. Exercising your senses is done by studying the Bible. By studying the written Word of God, you are learning how God thinks. It is by this means that your senses are exercised to discern the quiet voice of God. Knowing God's written will is the key to knowing God's un-written will.

This is how to distinguish God's voice by faith from the other thoughts in your mind. If this idea seems unclear to you, try it yourself. Study the Bible and pray to discover God's obvious will, apply it, and teach it. Eventually, you will recognize the quiet voice of God more consistently.

CONTENTMENT IN GOD'S WILL

I believe that doing God's will is the best thing you can do in life. He has the blueprints of your design and knows what is best for you. It is obvious from the problems in the world that humanity does not know better than God. The words of Jesus in the Garden of Gethsemane "not my will, but thine" should be the mantra of everyone who wants to live the best life possible.

Whatever God's will is, that is my will. I want whatever God wants for me. I am not aware of all that God has planned for me in this life, which includes sharing in the experiences of a world of sin and sorrows. But I am aware of what He plans for me in heaven, which does not include pain and sorrows. This is God's ultimate goal for me, for you, and for everyone else. And it will be a goal successfully reached, if we believe Him.

As for sharing in the sorrows of this world, I am not a medical statistic. I am God's statistic. I trust Him with my life and my plans. I do not want to miss the opportunities to be used by God. I want to see God's plan for my life. This requires believing Him, listening to Him, and obeying Him.

He granted my prayers to understand prayers that move mountains. This is what I wanted to know. I had no doubt that is what God wanted me to know, and He granted my request with the best answer for me to learn by.

In Philippians 4:11, Paul says, "Not that I speak in respect of want: for I have learned, in whatsoever state I am, therewith to be content." Being content with whatever occurs in your life comes with trusting God. If you are content in accepting God's will, your life at all times will be a testimony to others of how worthy God is to be served.

Being content is not an excuse for being lazy and unambitious. Contentment means to be accepting of the circumstances of life. It does not mean that you cannot change your circumstances. It does not mean that you should not make plans or develop skills to serve God better. It does not mean that you accept staying right where you are. Contentment is being thankful to the Lord at any moment of your life.

After Paul and Silas were falsely accused, wrongfully charged, humiliated, beaten, and cast into jail with their feet in stocks, at midnight they prayed and sang praises to God (Acts 16:25). How were these men able to praise God after all the injustice and pain they suffered? Why were they not fretting? Why were they not complaining? Why were they not angry? The answer is simple. They were content. They were doing God's will, and they were experiencing the repercussions of serving God. It would have been a contradiction to their message of God's love and worthiness if they had been complaining.

Jesus told His disciples in John 15:18, "If the world hate you, ye know that it hated me before it hated you." And He said in Matthew 5:11, "Blessed are ye, when men shall revile you, and persecute you, and shall say all manner of evil against you falsely, for my sake." Paul and Silas were blessed in serving God. Their blessing was not in being in pain-free comfort and joy. Their blessing was in being identified with Christ and serving Him. They were in good company with their Savior. Their persecution was not desirable, but it was no surprise. They knew that they lived in a world rebelling against God but that they were in good hands. God was in control, and for this reason, they were content and at peace.

Though they were content in jail, they still prayed. What do you think they prayed for? I have no doubt they prayed for their safety, health, and well-being. And based on Paul's testimony throughout all of his letters, he was praying for the salvation of the jailor, for the other prisoners, for other saints, and for mission efforts to reach the world with the Gospel. Paul and Silas were content but praying for change at the same time. God was in control, so whatever He allowed was acceptable to them.

The Apostle Peter and other disciples were also content in their ministries in spite of imprisonment, beatings, and threats. Acts 5:41 says, "…they departed from the presence of the council, rejoicing that they were counted worthy to suffer shame for his name."

Obviously, being beaten and imprisoned was a part of the ministry experience for the apostles and other followers of Christ. And though persecution was expected, and though they were content with whatever God allowed, they prayed for change in their circumstances. Acts 12:5 says, "Peter therefore was kept in prison: but prayer was made without ceasing of the church unto God for him." The believers prayed. They did not complain. They were content.

Contentment comes with knowing that God's will is good, perfect, and acceptable. There is no reason to blame God for the suffering that occurs in the world. We have no one to blame but ourselves.

Our contentment is a good testimony of how worthy God is. Complaining that God does not care about us is a false accusation. Suffering and sorrows are caused by those who reject God and His will. His compassion and power are not determined by our comfort and ease. He is not less powerful or less loving because He does not do things as we or others would. He knows what He is doing.

I find it remarkable how irrational it is to complain against God. We choose not to listen to God. We choose to do things our own way. Then when problems occur, we complain that God does not care. It makes no sense to blame God for the consequences of our choices, especially when He has warned us of the consequences.

There is no reason to blame God for the suffering that occurs in the world. We have no one to blame but ourselves.

The irrationality of complaint against God is rooted in selfishness, which keeps people perpetually discontent. Subsequently, we live in a culture of anger, bitterness, and hate. Jesus, Peter, Paul, and many others showed compassion and demonstrated lifestyles of being helpful. Their message was one of peace with God and with others. In return, they were despised and hated. They were treated harshly in spite of their message. We truly live in an irrational and perverse world.

As I explained before, sinners are to blame for suffering in the world. That means all of humanity is to blame, because no one is without sin.

The consequences of sin are predictable outcomes of sin. God has warned us since the beginning of time of the dangers and harm of sin. But we choose to do things our own way; so the consequences and blame are ours to own.

Because suffering is inevitable in this world, we as believers cannot escape the evils. But we can escape the personal feelings of anger and bitterness that come with discontentment. Rather than complain, we can show that God's grace is sufficient.

Suffering in our lives is a warning that no one can escape the dangerous consequences of sin. Contentment while suffering is a testimony of our trust in Christ, that He is doing that which is ultimately good. Romans 8:28 says, "And we know that all things work together for good to them that love God, to them who are the called according to his purpose."

WHAT CAUSES CANCER?

If you are like most, when you have a problem, you like to find what the cause is so you can find a solution. This is especially true when you are feeling very sick or facing a life-threatening disease like cancer. Knowledge is power in that it can help you make good decisions to reduce your risk of getting sick and to find a cure for your problem.

Scientists like to find the cause of problems for the same reasons. The current research shows that the cause of Hodgkin's lymphoma is still unknown. The Epstein Barr virus is sometimes mentioned as a possible suspect, but most people who have been infected never get Hodgkin's. Other risk factors include age, gender, family history, and a weakened immune system. But none are conclusive. No genes have been associated with it.

If you are suffering from cancer, you are probably wondering why. Cancer can occur for any number of reasons. To begin with, cancer refers to the condition of cells that multiply without inhibition. Normal cells multiply but are inhibited from continual replication. What inhibits cells from uncontrolled growth? It is genetic control. If the genes responsible for controlling cell growth are damaged, then the cell will multiply and not stop. A mass of cells may accumulate and form a tumor. Other cells, such as blood cells, accumulate throughout the body but do not form a hard tumor because they are loose cells or in soft tissue.

Genes in your cells control what cells do and ultimately what you do by producing proteins called enzymes. Enzymes determine what activities your cells can or cannot do. If the proteins responsible for controlling cellular multiplication are not produced, your cells will continue to multiply. They will not stop. These cells will replace or crowd out normal cells. A tumor of uncontrolled growing cells can put pressure on blood vessels and restrict blood flow. Or a tumor in the brain might create pressure inside the skull and kill normal cells by the increasing pressure.

What causes gene damage that prevents control of cell replication? The causes are grouped into four categories: 1) radiation, 2) chemical, 3) mechanical, and 4) biological. *Radiation* from the sun, from x-ray machines, from radioactive elements, from tanning booths, and more is absorbed by cells. The energy from the radiation excites electrons in molecules and can cause chemical reactions. *Chemicals* absorbed from the environment such as gasoline, benzene, tobacco smoke or chew, and more can enter into cells and react with the DNA molecule to damage genes. *Mechanical* causes usually involve microscopic slivers that can pierce the cell membrane without killing the cell. For example, fiberglass or asbestos slivers breathed into your lungs can penetrate your skin and lung cells and physically damage the DNA molecule. *Biologically,* an infection with a virus can cause cancer because viruses invade cells and embed themselves into the DNA molecules. Insertion of the virus into the wrong spot (some spots in the DNA are more harmful than others) can damage the gene that controls cell replication. There are many more examples. But the point is that there are so many causes for cancer that patients must be evaluated individually for cause and appropriate treatment.

Considering these causes of cancer leaves the impression that cancer is inevitable and inescapable. It is. Cancer is a product of ordinary cellular activity. We all have cancer during our lifetime. Why? Mistakes happen. Over 100 trillion cells in your body are maintaining their health by chemical reactions called metabolism. The DNA molecules in every cell are being replicated and transcribed at all times. With over 100 trillion cells in your body metabolizing every second of each day, there are trillions of opportunities for mistakes to occur every second of your life.

You might be wondering that, if everyone has cancer at some time in life, then why are there so many who do not die from cancer? Your cells are designed with the remarkable ability to correct most of the mistakes that occur. Correcting genetic errors helps to *prevent* out-of-control growth of cells. Your immune system helps to *remove* out-of-control cells from your body and is designed to identify and destroy those cells that fail to correct their genetic corruptions. For most people, both of these activities prevent cancer from overtaking their bodies. It is important to do things that promote good health and avoid doing things that put you at risk.

Some things that can be done to reduce the risk of suffering from cancer include reducing your exposure to things that are known to cause cancer. For example, use sun tan lotion. Stay away from radioactive elements. Keep your immune system strong by getting sufficient rest, observing a healthy diet, and exercising. Asking your doctor to screen you for known cancer-causing mutations will help catch cancer early enough to treat it. Regular examinations are good for catching problems early in the disease stage.

Some things are unavoidable, like getting older. The older we get, the more our cells have replicated and metabolized. Just the sheer number of metabolic cycles over time increases the probability of mistakes. And with age, the effectiveness of the immune system diminishes. This means our defense against wayward cells is not as good as it was in our younger days. The probability of cancer cells overwhelming our defense systems increases with age.

In my case, as with many other lymphomas, there is no known cause, and so specific preventive measures are not known. But reducing risks for specific cancers can help reduce the risk of all cancers, especially if we are doing things to boost our immune system.

But there are some things you inherit genetically that you can do nothing about. You are born that way. This is the case with your nature. Your nature is your moral compass. Your nature dictates the morality of your thoughts, motives, and behavior. The Bible says that human nature is sinful and that you were born with this sin nature (Romans 3:10; Psalm 51:5).

You sin because you have a sin nature. The Law of God reveals your sin nature by describing sinful thoughts and deeds. If you are guilty of sin, then you have a sin nature. This diagnosis lets you know that you need to be born again. You need a new nature. This is impossible for you to do, but nothing is impossible for God. And His desire is to change you if you give Him permission to do so. All you have to do is believe that He will. The remedy will be instantly applied, and you will be born again as a new person.

Jesus describes this new birth in John 3:3, saying, "… Verily, verily, I say unto thee, Except a man be born again, he cannot see the kingdom of God." He continues by saying in verse 6, "That which is born of the flesh is flesh; and that which is born of the Spirit is spirit." You are born again spiritually, not physically. The nature of your physical body remains unchanged. This is the reason you continue to experience the impulses to sin. As a believer, these impulses come from your physical body, not from your spirit. Your spirit desires to do right because, being born again, it has a new nature. As a believer, it is important to train your body to follow the impulses of your spirit in order to experience God's blessings and plan for your life.

Scientists are still searching for the cause of some cancers like Hodgkin's lymphoma. But regardless of the cause, for me, God used it for a purpose. I cannot say that I would not have had cancer if I had not prayed to understand prayers that move mountains. But I can say that God used it to help me understand how mountains are moved.

SEARCHING FOR A SOLUTION

While waiting for the test results, I went to the hospital library to read articles about Hodgkin's lymphoma. I searched and read all the medical articles I could find on treating the disease. Not surprisingly, they all said the same thing. The cause was unknown; the stages were clearly defined; and the treatment, depending on the stage of the cancer, could be radiation, surgery, chemotherapy, or a combination of these.

The drugs used for chemotherapy were Mechlorethamine Hydrochloride (nitrogen mustard), Oncovin® (Vincristine Sulfate), Prednisone (a steroid to reduce inflammation), and Procarbazine. The acronym for these four drugs is MOPP.

I interviewed a man in a nearby town who had been treated for Hodgkin's lymphoma with MOPP ten years earlier, and he was still spending most of his time in bed. His wife came home from work every day and checked on him first thing to see if he was still breathing. He said the chemo had left him chronically weakened. I was determined to find an alternative if at all possible.

I was encouraged to contact doctors in other countries who claimed to be able to cure cancers. I contacted a doctor in Greece because a group of patients living near me said they had been successfully treated. I called the doctor. After a thirty-minute interview of questions, the nurse asked me again what kind of cancer I had. After I told her again, she told me that their treatment would not help me.

The main question I was asking and not getting an answer to was what their fail rate was. They could tell me that they had successes, but those people were not available to talk to. A hundred success stories sound great, but this was out of how many patients treated? Was this a 100 percent cure rate or a 1 percent cure rate? I kept asking for this information until the nurse finally told me that they would not be able to treat my type of cancer.

The Bible warns of false prophets preying on people desperate for hope and healing.

Spiritually, the Bible speaks of false prophets and false messages. Many claim to have the power to heal. Others hold out promises that healing is possible. But the result is disillusionment, unfulfilled promises. Some might really think they can heal, but most, I believe, are fakes.

The Bible warns of false prophets preying on people desperate for hope and healing. It is cruel to treat desperately sick people this way. But that is the way of Satan and his followers.

False prophets offer false messages of salvation, but there is only one true message that can save your soul. I remember the first time I experienced conviction about my dilemma with sin and condemnation. This was an experience of faith in action. God revealed to me that I had a problem and needed a cure.

I was sharing a house with three other guys all attending UC Irvine. We were all members of the same Christian ministry. I was reading Matthew 7, and verses 1–2 say, "Judge not, that ye be not judged. For with what judgment ye judge, ye shall be judged: and with what measure ye mete, it shall be measured to you again." I immediately felt convicted about my sin and impending judgment. So I thought, *Based on this verse, God will judge me more leniently if I am lenient with others.* Then I had to think about how leniently I wanted to be judged by God. I concluded that I wouldn't judge anyone at all so that God would not judge me. But I was still troubled about being judged, so I asked one of my roommates what the verse meant. He said he didn't know.

I read further and was challenged by verses 13–14, which say, "Enter ye in at the strait gate: for wide is the gate, and broad is the way, that leadeth to destruction, and many there be which go in thereat: Because strait is the gate, and narrow is the way, which leadeth unto life, and few there be that find it." I had always thought differently. I thought God would save most people, except for those who were just flat out evil. But this verse says that most people will choose the wrong path.

I later learned that Jesus was talking to people who were trying to get to heaven by impressing God with their sincerity and good behavior. It is the inclination of man to want to do something in order to be worthy of God's rewards. They cannot accept the fact that they cannot impress God and that He deserves all the credit for showing grace without regard to any merit of goodness on their part. If they could be good enough to deserve a reward, then God would owe them a reward. But it is impossible for God to owe anyone. I don't think most people realize this implication of a reward-based religion. But some people invent religions to make them feel good about themselves. Sadly, they will discover they were wrong, and then they will not feel good.

As you probably have noticed, many people think themselves experts on religion. I am amazed at how many I meet who have strong opinions about the Bible, even though most have never read it, much less studied it. But such is the way of mankind. And for this reason, most prefer to follow their own way rather than God's way. This is the reason the way to condemnation is broad.

Most religious views are legalistic and involve self-righteous judgments of others. Legalists are those who believe that salvation requires keeping the Law. They use the Law to judge the righteousness or unrighteousness of themselves and others. In Matthew 7:1–2, Jesus warned that those who judge will be judged. Jesus was telling them that those who try to live by the Law will be judged by the Law. And the Bible is very clear that those who live by the Law will die by the Law. They will not be saved by the Law (Romans 3:28).

To live by the Law means to be dependent upon the Law for righteousness and salvation. But this is the wrong approach to being righteous. As I have already mentioned, the Law was given to show people that they are sinners, not to make them righteous. Galatians 3:11 says, "But that no man is justified by the law in the sight of God, it is evident: for, The just shall live by faith."

Most legalists do not deny the importance of being saved by God's grace because the Bible says salvation is by grace. The problem is that they try to combine their works with God's grace. But the definition of grace prevents combining the grace of God with the works of men. Romans 11:6 says, "And if by grace, then is it no more of works: otherwise grace is no more grace. But if it be of works, then is it no more grace: otherwise work is no more work." In other words, whatever is by grace must be *only* by grace. Works are not and cannot be involved. They are mutually exclusive. And if something is by works, then it must be only by works. It cannot involve grace.

> *Whatever is by grace must be only by grace. Works are not and cannot be involved.*

Religions that rely on works or on works plus grace do not lead people to God. They lead people to their own religious opinions. Almost all religions teach people to rely on their sincerity and good works to go to heaven. This is the broad way. They rely on the Law and works for reward from God rather than on promise and repentance for grace from God.

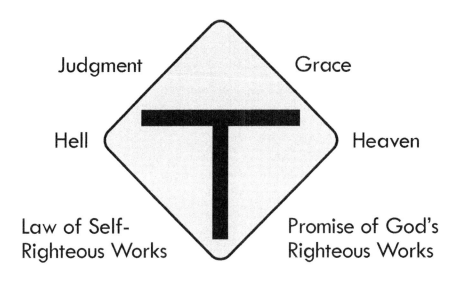

Judgment   Grace

Hell   Heaven

Law of Self-Righteous Works   Promise of God's Righteous Works

But Jesus said in John 14:6, "… I am the way, the truth, and the life: no man cometh unto the Father, but by me." Jesus is the only way to heaven. He is the only door and the only pathway leading to God. He is the one who does all the work and gets all the credit for saving souls. No one is capable of saving himself or is worthy enough to be saved. Salvation is possible only because of the mercy and grace of God. He promises salvation as a free gift because it cannot be obtained by any other means. Jesus alone makes this gift possible, and so salvation is His way and only His way. Acts 4:12 says, "Neither is there salvation in any other: for there is none other name under heaven given among men, whereby we must be saved." This is the narrow way because there is only one way to God and heaven.

God has given us His written Word, His Spirit, and His church to protect us from deception and frauds. If you study His Word, pray for understanding, and listen to God's teachers in His churches, you will find the narrow way that leads to life everlasting.

1989 STAGING CANCER

During my initial visit with the oncologist Dr. Hayward in March of 1989, Colleen and I spent forty-five minutes asking him questions about my disease, treatment, and prognosis. He answered each one patiently and sat with us until we were done.

Dr. Hayward was known for being a good doctor. My cousin, a cardiologist in Batesville, Arkansas, checked out Dr. Hayward for me. I was trying to decide whether to go to the Duke University Medical Center, M.D. Anderson, Sloan and Kettering, the Mayo Clinic, or stay in Fayetteville. I wanted to get treated successfully by knowledgeable doctors. Dr. Hayward was the only oncologist in Fayetteville and one of two in the area at the time. My cousin told me that Dr. Hayward had an excellent reputation and was a great choice.

My review of the medical literature on cancer showed that about 3 out of 100,000 people in the U.S., mostly men, are affected by Hodgkin's lymphoma. There was a standard protocol for staging and treating the cancer, so I was not concerned about needing a doctor who was knowledgeable about new and innovative methods of treatment for Hodgkin's lymphoma. During the initial interview with Dr. Hayward, he said he would work with anyone I preferred to consult with as my primary oncologist, regardless of their location.

I said to Dr. Hayward, "I was thinking about going to M.D. Anderson. What do you think?"

"They have an excellent reputation. If that's what you decide to do, that is fine. If you want to have them set up a treatment schedule for you, I'll be glad to do it here so you can stay in Fayetteville during the chemotherapy. Whatever you decide, I'll work with you."

I was impressed with Dr. Hayward's willingness to be a team player. I felt at liberty to talk to him without offending him and to ask all the questions that came to my mind. I chose to stay in Fayetteville.

I have read testimonies of others attending some of the larger medical centers, and they felt like a number, alienated, lonely, isolated, and just another patient paying the bills. I never felt that way in Dr. Hayward's office. Comparing my experience with others', I advise the more personal situation with a good doctor, if possible.

"What is the next step?" I asked Dr. Hayward.

"We need to determine the stage of your cancer. This will determine the course of treatment."

"How long will that take?"

"About a week to two weeks."

Usually, Hodgkin's lymphoma presents itself as a lump in the neck or in the armpit at the earliest stage. At stage 1, the cancer is limited to one area of lymph nodes. At stage 2, two or more sites of lymph nodes are involved, but only above or below the diaphragm. At stage 3, lymph node sites in the upper body and the lower body are involved. At stage 4, the cancer has escaped the lymph system and has spread to other parts of the body.

Dr. Hayward was hopeful that I was in stage 1 because this cancer can be treated successfully. An upper body computer tomography (CT) scan was scheduled for the next day. The day following the CT scan, Dr. Hayward told me that the lymph node sites under my sternum were swollen and involved. I was definitely a stage 2 at least. The CT scan did not show signs of swollen lymph nodes in my abdomen. However, surgery would be needed to determine stage 3. In this procedure, the doctor would explore the body cavity, examine the lymph node sites, and remove the spleen and swollen lymph nodes. This was protocol in 1989.

Dr. Hayward said to me, "Based on the CT scan, there is a good chance you are not stage 3. I suggest we rule out stage 4 before we do any surgery."

"Why is that?"

"If you are stage 4, then the course of action is determined, and you will not have to undergo surgery."

To determine stage 4, a bone marrow biopsy is done. This could be a very painful procedure, but Dr. Hayward used a mild sedative.

Under anesthesia, my short term memory was affected. During the procedure, I kept asking the nurse what her name was. I knew that I knew her, but I couldn't retain her name in my memory. Every time she told me her name, I would say, "Oh yes, I know you." I did that throughout the entire procedure. Colleen was in the room too, and she said the doctor, the nurse, and she were all laughing at me because I couldn't remember her name and kept asking. Later the nurse laughed when she told me that she had never seen a drunken preacher before.

When I fully awoke, I had two sore spots on the back of my hip bones. Two days later the results were in.

The results were not what we expected. My bone marrow was full of lymphoma cells. I had nodular sclerosing Hodgkin's lymphoma, stage 4, type B. This was not good news, but Dr. Hayward was optimistic and always positive when he talked to me.

Dr. Hayward told me the only treatment in my case was chemotherapy. Radiation and surgery would not be helpful. I was ready to start as soon as possible but needed to discuss everything with Colleen. The chemo treatments were scheduled every other week. I ended up choosing Mondays for my treatments so that I would have two full weeks to recover enough to attend every other Sunday service at church.

THE SCHOOL OF EXPERIENCE

Like many things, it is one thing to know about prayer. It is another to experience it. I spent twelve months studying and writing about prayer, but God had plans to extend my study through the experience of praying prayers to move my mountain. Through application, God taught me more than I had learned through book study.

Through study of His Word, I discovered the importance of knowing what it means to have faith in God. Through experience, I learned the importance of friendship with God. His presence and comfort during my time of chemotherapy were truly amazing.

The experience of moving this mountain in my life involved more than just gaining insights about prayer. There were multiple lessons learned. Prayers specifically granted by God often come with multiple benefits. This is the reason that throughout this book much more is shared than just insights into prayer.

I had asked God many times to teach me without taking the time to guide me through learning experiences. God does give insights into His Word through revelation, but often it requires time and experiences to really learn the lessons. His lesson for me was to take me through the experience of prayer so that I could experience it firsthand.

GREAT INSIGHTS TO REMEMBER

1. Prayer is for our benefit, not God's.
2. The cause of sinfulness is the human nature of sin.
3. The nature of sin must be changed by the miraculous work of God.
4. Fear not knowing God's will.
5. The quiet voice of God is discernible.

6. God made us intelligent to ask questions and to learn.

7. Praying for God's will to be done in your life is not a request to suffer.

8. Knowing God's written will is the key to knowing God's unwritten will.

9. If you are content in accepting God's will, your life at all times will be a testimony to others of how worthy God is to be served.

10. There is one narrow path to God because there is only one God who did all the work to make the cure for sin possible.

11. God uses time and experiences to teach us.

2
PRAYING FOR WHAT I WANT

But I know, that even now, whatsoever thou wilt ask of God,
God will give it thee.
—John 11:22

I do not recall ever being hesitant about praying for something, even trivial things. My prayers range from asking for help to find a pencil in the house to requesting relief from a headache, from finding a parking spot to understanding a verse. I pray about everything and anything.

I thank God for the food I eat with an intense sense of gratefulness. First Timothy 4:4–5 says, "For every creature of God is good, and nothing to be refused, if it be received with thanksgiving: For it is sanctified by the word of God and prayer."

Some might think that having food to eat, especially in a culture suffering from obesity, is trivial, but not me. I am thankful to God for everything I have and experience in my life.

Though God is the Creator of the entire universe, no request is too trivial to Him. Jesus explains in Luke 12:6–7 that God is attentive to every detail in our lives, saying, "Are not five sparrows sold for two farthings, and not one of them is forgotten before God? But even the very hairs of your head are all numbered. Fear not therefore: ye are of more value than many sparrows." Nothing in God's creation is unimportant to Him. No detail is too insignificant to Him. Anything you are concerned about, He is concerned about.

I enjoy watching my grandson play with toys or look at his fingers with great curiosity. It is fun to play peek-a-boo with him and share his repeated amazement at a floating feather in air. When he holds up a tiny thread of string to show me what he has, I act amazed. Why? It is important to him. And because it is important to him, it is important to me. I love him. This is how it is with God. He loves us. And anything important to us is important to Him.

This does not mean that everything is of equal importance. Nothing is more important than the salvation of a soul. But to God, the importance of a soul does not make everything else unimportant.

Philippians 4:6 says, "Be careful for nothing; but in every thing by prayer and supplication with thanksgiving let your requests be made known unto God." To be "careful for nothing" means to not be anxious about anything. Don't worry about anything. If you have a concern about something, talk to God about it. It does not matter what it is that you are concerned about or how many things you are concerned about. Talk to Him.

You cannot keep secrets from God, so you might as well just talk to Him about whatever is on your mind.

It is funny to ponder what to talk to God about, as if He doesn't already know. He already knows what you are thinking, what you worry about, and what you do or do not want to talk to Him about. He is listening to every thought in your mind. And further, Jesus says in Matthew 6:8, "… your Father knoweth what things ye have need of, before ye ask him." You cannot keep secrets from God, so you might as well just talk to Him about whatever is on your mind.

You can talk to God about anything. Nothing is too trivial to pray about. No request is too small or unimportant. And He wants you to talk to Him.

WANTING WHAT GOD WANTS

I discovered that frustration and disappointment with praying can be greatly reduced when prayers are offered in God's will. This means adjusting your wants to conform to His wants. When your desires are His desires, then anything you pray for will be granted.

Obviously, it is wrong to think that praying for whatever you want means without regard for what is right. God does not condone sin, so He is not going to grant prayers for sin. He is not going to grant prayers to help you steal, cheat, defraud others, or to do anything that would promote evil. He is not going to grant prayers that do not align with His will to fulfill His purpose of saving souls.

In John 9:31, a blind man who had been healed by Jesus said, "Now we know that God heareth not sinners: but if any man be a worshipper of God, and doeth his will, him he heareth." David also said in Psalm 66:18, "If I regard iniquity in my heart, the Lord will not hear me."

Does God not hear the prayers of sinners? How is it possible for an all-knowing God not to hear the prayers of sinners? And how does God save a sinner's soul if He does not know the thoughts and hear the prayers of sinners? The statement that God *does not hear* the prayers of sinners is an expression meaning that God *does not grant* the requests of sinners. He *does not regard* their requests because they have no regard for Him. God hears their prayers and knows what they want, but he does not grant their prayers.

When Jesus said to ask for whatever was desired, He was talking to those who loved Him and wanted to follow. Permission from God to pray for whatever is desired is to those who love Him and live for Him. These are the people we must identify with if we want permission to ask for whatever we want. Those who love God desire what He desires. They want what He wants. It is this kind of person Jesus was talking to. This is the kind of person we must be.

Most of the verses in the Bible that talk about praying for whatever you want include a qualifying statement such as have faith, desire God, pray in Christ's name, obey His commands, and pray according to His will. This explains why some prayers are granted and others are not. *You can ask whatever you want, but you will receive only that which does not violate God's will.*

You can ask whatever you want, but you will receive only that which does not violate God's will.

When Christ told His disciples to ask for whatever they wanted, He was talking to people who loved and followed Him. Their desire was to fulfill Christ's desire. They did His bidding.

They wanted what He wanted.

In John 14:13–14, Jesus says, "And whatsoever ye shall ask in my name, that will I do, that the Father may be glorified in the Son. If ye shall ask any thing in my name, I will do it." Asking in the name of Christ is asking for things He would ask for. "In Christ's name" is not a command statement. No one can demand of God that He grant a request because a prayer ends with the words "In Christ's name."

People claiming Christ's authority to demand that something be done as they request are more often disappointed than not. They do not get whatever they ask for. Obviously, they did not pray in Jesus' name, as they said with their words.

> *God will give you whatever you want when you want what He wants.*

To ask in Christ's name is to ask that His will be done. You are His representative. You do not represent yourself. To ask for anything in His name indicates that you are requesting only that which is acceptable to Him. You want His purpose fulfilled. In other words, God will give you whatever you want when you want what He wants.

How do you acquire the right to pray and preach in the name of Christ? He grants it to you. Anyone can claim it. But only those who walk with God receive it. First John 5:14–15 explains, "And this is the confidence that we have in him, that, if we ask any thing according to his will, he heareth us: And if we know that he hear us, whatsoever we ask, we know that we have the petitions that we desired of him." When our requests are in agreement with God's will, they will be granted.

In John 15:7, Jesus says, "If ye abide in me, and my words abide in you, ye shall ask what ye will, and it shall be done unto you." To abide in Christ means to be in fellowship with Him. You not only know what His will is, but you want His will to be done. This means that your prayer requests align with His will. Those who ask according to His will, receive.

KNOWING GOD'S WILL

My prayer experiences were not the same as what I was reading in the Bible, so I asked God to show me what I was doing wrong. I wanted to pray the right way according to His will.

I discovered that there are three reasons for not knowing God's will. First, God did not tell you. Second, God told you, but you were not listening. Third, you did not ask.

Is it possible *not* to know God's will even though you are committed to serving Him? Yes. God does not tell us all the details of His plan for our lives. He does not reveal everything there is to know about His will all the time. However, He does reveal what is necessary for us to know.

The Apostle Paul desired to do God's will. He was committed to serving Christ, but he had to be corrected in his plans. He was making plans to go to Asia Minor for his third missionary journey. But the Holy Ghost prevented him. Acts 16:6–7 says, "Now when they had gone throughout Phrygia and the region of Galatia, and were forbidden of the Holy Ghost to preach the word in Asia, After they were come to Mysia, they assayed to go into Bithynia: but the Spirit suffered them not." They were forbidden by the Holy Ghost to preach in Asia. They attempted to go to Bithynia and again were prevented by the Spirit of God. Why did they attempt to go places that God did not want them to go? Paul was preaching the Gospel of salvation, training disciples, and organizing churches. He was not in rebellion to God.

This is a good example to show that God does not reveal His entire plan. He reveals His plan on a need to know basis. Paul was doing what God had sent him to do (Acts 13:2–7). As soon as the

Holy Spirit revealed to him to change the location of his ministry, Paul did it. He was listening and eager to hear God's voice. He wanted to do God's will.

There are details about God's will for our lives that He does not reveal. They are not necessary for us to know in order to serve Him. The details He is willing to show us at any given moment are sufficient.

A second reason for not knowing God's will is failure to listen to God. Some do not want to listen to Him. More than likely, they are glad not to know His will. Their will and wants are more important to them than God's. Their concerns and desires are not His, so they fear what He might ask them to do. Because they are unwilling to sacrifice their ambitions and goals for Him, they refuse to hear God's will for their lives. There are no rewards for those who do not listen to God.

A third reason for not knowing God's will is failure to ask. God is willing to reveal some things to us, but He requires that we ask. If we do not ask, then we do not know. James 1:5 says, "If any of you lack wisdom, let him ask of God, that giveth to all men liberally, and upbraideth not; and it shall be given him." This applies to everyone. No one automatically possesses the wisdom necessary to know and to do God's will. But to have wisdom, we must ask God to grant it to us. Only the proud think they have no need to ask God for wisdom. Those who do not ask remain ignorant.

All you have to do is desire to know His will, ask, and listen.

Ask the Lord to teach you about knowing His will. Ask Him to help you to understand His Word, to love Him more, to abide in Him, to pray better, and to serve Him. All you have to do is desire to know His will, ask, and listen.

PRAYING THE RIGHT WAY

If you do not know God's will, it is important to discover why you do not know. Could it be that God has already revealed enough? Could it be you have not asked? Or could it be you are not listening? If you are doing right, asking, and listening, then God has told you all that you need to know. But what if you are asking and trying to listen, and you are doing what you know is right, yet you still do not know God's will? Examine how you are asking.

If you are asking God to reveal His will to you, and you feel frustrated because you are not receiving an answer, it may be that you are not praying right. There are three minimum requirements for praying the right way. These three requirements are *faith, belief,* and *righteousness.* This means that praying the right way requires being a born-again believer, living for God, and believing in whatever God reveals that you should pray for.

I knew in 1988 by faith that the promises in God's Word were given to be understood and experienced. So I prayed to understand and experience the prayers that move mountains. I believed that I could submit this request to God, and I was confident that He would grant my request. I was committed to living for Him and desired that His will be done in my life. Like I said before, I did not pray for cancer. Such an experience was not even on my mind. God chose to use cancer to teach me about prayers that move mountains.

God's way is always the right way to pray. Praying with any other perspective leads to frustration and disappointment. God, as the Creator of all things, created the rules of how things should be done. He created the laws that govern the universe. He created the laws that govern our relationship with Him. He created the rules for how to pray. He knows what is best. He never makes mistakes.

To pray the right way, you need faith, belief, and righteousness. You need to know by faith what you can pray for. You need to believe that you can pray for it. And you must offer your prayers in righteousness. By fulfilling these three requirements of prayer, you can know that God's will is being done.

RIGHTEOUS PRAYERS

The third minimum requirement of prayer, which is righteousness, has two criteria. First, to pray right, you must *be* right. Second, to pray right, you must *live* right. To be right, you must be saved. To live right, you must be sanctified.

Salvation is God's work to make you righteous so you can *be* right. Sanctification is *your* work to *live* right. God's work is perfect and will never fail. Your work will never be perfect. God makes your inward, spiritual man righteous. This is a miraculous change that secures your soul forever with eternal life. You, in contrast, are tasked with the responsibility to make your outward body of flesh *do* right. The choices you make will be judged to determine your rewards and losses. Your imperfections and struggles as a Christian should make you very thankful that your salvation is based on the promise and work of God, not on your works.

Sometimes people confuse acting righteous with being righteous. But acting or looking righteous does not make you righteous.

Jesus challenged the Pharisees about their appearance of being righteous, saying in Matthew 23:28, "Even so ye also outwardly appear righteous unto men, but within ye are full of hypocrisy and iniquity." Jesus said they looked righteous because they acted righteous. They were hypocrites. Hypocrisy is claiming to be something you are not. The Pharisees were hypocrites because they acted like they knew God and claimed to *be* righteous. But they were not righteous. They were unrighteous. Acting righteous did not make them righteous. They were unrighteous because they were not born again. Doing what is right does not make you right. This is what I mean when I say to pray right, you must be right as well as live right.

Let me clarify that doing wrong is not okay if you are not born again and righteous. It is always right and best to do right. But doing what is righteous will not make you righteous.

BEING RIGHTEOUS

Being right is to be right with God. This requires the miraculous work of God to make you righteous. You must literally be made righteous. Your nature, your being, what you are must be changed by God. Jesus called this being born again. He must make you brand new, from scratch. This is called spiritual birth, in contrast to physical birth. This is what it takes to be saved. Jesus said in John 3:5–7, "... Verily, verily, I say unto thee, Except a man be born of water and [of] the Spirit, he cannot enter into the kingdom of God. That which is born of the flesh is flesh; and that which is born of the Spirit is spirit. Marvel not that I said unto thee, Ye must be born again." There is a physical birth and a spiritual birth. When you are born of your parents, you are a body, soul, and spirit. When you are born again of God the moment you believe Him, He changes you spiritually. When He returns from heaven, He will change your body. It is your birth that determines your nature. Your parents passed on to you the unrighteous nature inherited from Adam. The only way to have a righteous nature is by being born again of God.

HOW TO BE BORN AGAIN AND RIGHTEOUS

We call on the Lord for salvation because we desire to be saved not only from condemnation, but also from the control of sin. This is called repentance. Repentance is a change of mind. The moment you change your mind to believe God, you have repented. To believe in God is to believe His way is the right way. It is accepting His way as the right way for you. You trust Him and accept His will for your life. This change in *belief* from your way to God's way is repentance.

Desiring the benefits of God's way is not believing. It is possible to desire God's blessings and want to believe but still be unwilling to *trust* God and to *accept* His way. This is a conflict of desires. It is possible to *desire* to believe and be blessed and also to *desire* to continue to live your own way. Acts 26:28 records an example of this conflict of desires, saying, "Then Agrippa said unto Paul, Almost thou persuadest me to be a Christian." Agrippa had the desire to believe but was also reluctant about believing. He chose not to believe Paul's message. He was almost persuaded to believe, but he decided not to accept God's message. *Almost* believing will not result in salvation.

The Apostle Paul explained this conflict between two desires as worldly sorrow and godly sorrow. He wrote in Second Corinthians 7:10, "For godly sorrow worketh repentance to salvation not to be repented of: but the sorrow of the world worketh death." Worldly sorrow is the desire to enjoy the blessings of God without accepting the will of God for your life. Godly sorrow is the desire to trust God and to accept His will for your life because you believe Him. Godly sorrow results in repentance, a change of mind or decision to trust God and accept His will as the right way for your life.

BELIEVING

One last point to make about *believing* is that there is a difference between believing that there is a God and believing that God is your God. James 2:19 says, "Thou believest that there is one God; thou doest well: the devils also believe, and tremble." The devils are not saved, yet they believe there is one God. They believe in God. They know Him. They have been in heaven with Him. But believing there is a God does not mean they believe Him and accept His will. They believe *in* God, but they do not believe Him. They did not change their minds to accept God's will as the best way for them. They chose their own will.

God answers our prayers for salvation the moment we believe Him by changing us spiritually. He literally makes us new and righteous by nature. As I mentioned before, this is a spiritual change, not a physical change in the body of flesh. This is a miracle that we are not capable of doing. Jesus says in John 1:13 about those who receive Him and are born as sons of God that they "… were born, not of blood, nor of the will of the flesh, nor of the will of man, but of God." New birth and imputed righteousness is all because of God. We must be saved His way, not our way. Do you believe this?

LIVING RIGHT

Once we are born of God, saved, and delivered from the control of sin as we desired, we can live right and pray right. With the righteousness of the new, inward man, the help of the Holy Spirit, fellowship with God, and His resources to help us, we can control sin rather than let sin control us. We can obey God and enjoy the life of blessings that He intended for us. As born-again believers, we can experience freedom from the control of sin.

Those who do not want to be delivered from sin's control over them do not repent. But without repentance, not only is there no deliverance from sin's control, but there is no deliverance from condemnation either. Jesus said in Luke 13:3, "I tell you, Nay: but, except ye repent, ye shall all likewise perish."

Repentance means that you decide to believe that God is right and you are wrong. To be *unrepentant* means that you don't believe God's way is the best way. It does *not* mean that you will necessarily live a debased lifestyle of sin.

> Repentance is when you decide to believe God is right and you are wrong.

There are three paths the unrepentant can take. The first is to live a vulgar lifestyle of indulging the lusts to sin without regard for right or wrong. The second is to live a religious lifestyle they deem good enough to impress God. The third path is to try to live a lifestyle good enough to impress others, religious or not. All paths of the unrepentant are choices to do things their own way, not God's way.

Because of the inward, spiritual change and the resources God gives to believers, they have the opportunity to experience the blessings of peace and love that come with living right. The more a believer obeys God, the more he will experience God's blessings. However, being changed and made righteous spiritually does not necessarily mean believers always live right. Born-again believers who choose to indulge the whims of the flesh rather than obey God do not enjoy the experiences God intended for them. These believers are called carnal Christians (First Corinthians 3:1).

Carnal Christians not only suffer the loss of blessings that come with living right, but they also will suffer loss when judged by God later.

First Corinthians 3:11–15 describes the judgment of Christians. This judgment is about rewards and loss. Born-again believers who are carnal do not revert to being *spiritually* unrighteous, so they cannot lose their salvation. Salvation is God's work, and eternal life is secure in Jesus Christ. The born-again, inward man of the believer cannot be unborn. The unrighteous works of the flesh cannot undo the righteous work of God spiritually. First Corinthians 3:15 says of those Christians who choose a life of carnality and disobedience, "If any man's work shall be burned, he shall suffer loss: but he himself shall be saved; yet so as by fire." Carnal Christians are saved, but they will suffer loss. Though they will suffer loss, they will not lose their salvation.

The fact that Christians will be judged for the lifestyles they choose means they are accountable to make the right choices. They can and should obey God. It is their loss if they choose otherwise. They will be rewarded if they choose to obey God.

Ephesians 2:8–10 explains that salvation is by God's work and grace without our works but that the Christian lifestyle is our responsibility. "For by grace are ye saved through faith; and that not of yourselves: it is the gift of God: Not of works, lest any man should boast. For we are his workmanship, created in Christ Jesus unto good works, which God hath before ordained that we should walk in them." Our salvation and new birth in righteousness is God's workmanship. Showing His workmanship in our lives is our responsibility.

Praying right requires being right and doing right. *Being* right requires being saved. This is God's work. *Doing* right is living right. This is our work. When God makes us right and we live right,

Praying the right way does not mean that you know exactly what to ask all the time.

then we want God's will to be done in our lives. At this point, we will pray the right way for the right things. And we can pray for whatever we want.

50

Praying the right way does not mean that we know exactly what to ask all the time. Many times we have to ask God for direction and answers. This also is the right way to pray.

LIVING RIGHT TO PRAY RIGHT

James 5:16 says that the prayers of a righteous man avail much. This means more than being made righteous through spiritual birth. It means that you live right. And if you live right, you pray right.

Jesus says in Luke 6:46, "And why call ye me, Lord, Lord, and do not the things which I say?" This challenge gets to the root of what kind of obedience God expects. Why do people want to call themselves Christians, claim that Jesus Christ is their Lord, and then disregard His will and lordship over their lives? This is called hypocrisy. I will clarify this idea of hypocrisy later in the chapter.

Living right is living God's way. This is obedience. *Saying* that you love God, that you obey God, and that you worship God does not make it so. You can say "Praise God." But are you praising Him? Jesus says in Matthew 15:8, "This people draweth nigh unto me with their mouth, and honoureth me with their lips; but their heart is far from me." *Saying* it and *doing* it are two different things. And saying you obey God is a lot easier than actually obeying Him.

Born-again Christians *want* to obey God. They agreed with God that it is good to escape from sin and to do right. They repented of their sins and asked to be delivered from sins in their lives. Salvation occurred the moment they believed God (John 5:24). God saved them as He promised. He gave them a new nature to preserve them. He also gave them three resources (the Word of God, the Spirit of God, and the church of God) to protect and train them. Individuals who *never* had a desire to escape sin and to do right, never truly repented. At best, they had a worldly sorrow, not a godly sorrow unto repentance. These individuals need to examine themselves to determine if they were ever truly saved.

Calling on God for salvation simply for "fire insurance" to escape condemnation is not repentance. This is very important to understand because Jesus says in Luke 13:3, "... except ye repent, ye shall all likewise perish." Repentance is a genuine desire for God to change you and deliver you from sin because you believe that God's way is the right way. You accept His way as your own. It makes no sense to return to sin after asking Him to deliver you from sin. We act on what we want like children wanting to eat ice cream. They ask for ice cream, and then, when it is given to them, they eat it. They really wanted it. If they refuse to eat it, then the parent asks, "You don't really want ice cream, do you?"

A righteous lifestyle is *the fruit* (result) of not only being born again with a new, righteous nature, but also being surrendered to do God's will. Some think righteous works and repentance are the same. But righteous works are not repentance. They are the fruit of repentance. They are the logical result of doing what you believe. You do what you believe is right. Believing God is repentance. What you do because you believe Him is the fruit of repentance.

Paul wrote in Romans 6:18–19, "Being then made free from sin, ye became the servants of righteousness. I speak after the manner of men because of the infirmity of your flesh: for as ye have yielded your members servants to uncleanness and to iniquity unto iniquity; even so now yield your members servants to righteousness unto holiness." If you truly called on God to deliver you from sin, then He has delivered you. So live like it. If you really wanted to be free from sin, then act like it. God did His part to deliver you from sin and permanently prevent your condemnation with the miracle of new birth. Now you are enabled to live free from the control of sin. It is the logical and reasonable thing to do if you have truly repented.

When individuals pray to the Lord only to be delivered from condemnation but have no desire to stop sinning, this is not repentance. They do not *believe* that God's way is the best way. There is no change in what they believe. But when they ask God to save them from sin and condemnation with a genuine desire to be delivered from sin, this is true repentance. This is what it means to believe God.

Genuine repentance results in salvation, which results in a righteous, inward man. This helps born-again believers control the sinful impulses of the outward, carnal body. They have a born-again spirit, God's resources, peer examples, and a genuine belief that controlling sin is better than letting sin control them. Paul wrote in Romans 6:21, "What fruit had ye then in those things whereof ye are now ashamed? for the end of those things is death." If you truly wanted to escape sin, then God has fulfilled His promise. He has made you righteous, has delivered you from the condemnation that comes because of sin, and has made it possible for you to control the sinful impulses in your body of flesh. By controlling these impulses, you can enjoy a better life in Christ's blessings, and you will pray right.

THE RIGHT MOTIVATION

It is always right to do right. It is never wrong to do right, and it is never right to do wrong. This is an important lesson to keep in mind because some Christians confuse *It is never wrong to do right, and it is never right to do wrong.* their feelings with their motivations. They are hesitant about doing good things because they do not *feel* like they have the right motivation.

Motivation is the reason behind what you do. The reason(s) could be emotional or rational or both. Whatever the reason might

53

be, motivation is the *why* behind what we do. The more compelling the reason, the more we are driven to do something.

As I mentioned before, the outward body of flesh does not always feel like doing what is right. So then, to do right often requires overriding the feelings of the flesh. What would compel someone to force himself to do right when he does not feel like it? A compelling reason. This compelling reason is his motivation, and this comes from the born-again, inward man, God's Word, and the Holy Spirit.

Being properly motivated to do right requires the right reason, namely, doing everything for God. Your flesh may not want to do right, but as long as you do right for the sake of obeying God, you are motivated correctly.

Being properly motivated does not mean the absence of negative feelings or the absence of selfish desires. It simply means that you want to obey God because it is the right thing to do regardless of your feelings.

Being properly motivated does not mean the absence of negative feelings or the absence of selfish desires.

The fact is your carnal body does not always want to do what is right. Its motives are often questionable. There is a conflict of two motives due to having a born-again spirit and a body that is not born again. When you choose to obey God and do right, you are properly motivated. Christians who force themselves to do right and obey God are obviously motivated enough, in a good way, to obey God in spite of the motivation and feelings in their flesh. This good motivation to do good comes from the inward, born-again spirit.

Rather than focus on the motivation from your body of flesh, focus on the motivation from your spirit and just do right. Paul said in Romans 7:21, "I find then a law, that, when I would do good, evil is present with me." Paul did not let the presence of evil in his body of flesh prevent him from obeying God. We should do likewise.

Satan wants you to be concerned about emotional motivation and the presence of negative motivations from your body of flesh. He wants to offer you excuses not to serve Christ. He wants you to focus on the feelings in your body of flesh, not those in your spirit. God, on the other hand, wants you to focus on the presence of the right motivation and ignore the presence of wrong motivations in your carnal body. He wants you to just do right.

You cannot always control how your body *feels*, but you can control what your body *does*. Without argument, it is easier to obey God when you feel like it. It feels a lot better to serve the Lord without the presence of evil and bad feelings. But as a born-again believer, you have a sense of responsibility to serve Christ regardless of your feelings. This sense of responsibility is the right reason to obey Him. This is the right motivation. When you experience conflicting desires and motivations, be encouraged, knowing that you have the right motivation when you choose to do right. As a born-again Christian, you will always have the right motivation regardless of what other wrong motivations might be present.

Do you think Jonah, a prophet of God, was properly motivated when he warned the citizens of Nineveh about the judgment of God? The Bible says he pouted and complained even after trying to run away from doing what God told him to do. But he eventually did it, and the result was favorable. Jonah was used of God in spite of his bad feelings and motivations. Why? Because he also had the right motivation.

I have heard people say that, if you do not have the right motivation, God is not pleased with what you do. It is true that

Being born-again means that God has ensured the presence of the right motivation at all times. God is not pleased with wrong motivations. But it is not true that Christians do not have the right motivation. Being born again means that God has ensured the presence of the right motivation at all times. For Christians, there is no excuse not to do right.

Having the right motivation present at all times does not mean that Christians do right all the time. It means that they have a choice to please God or not. They have a choice between doing right and wrong every day. They have a choice between the desires of the flesh and the desires of the spirit.

What should Christians do about the presence of wrong motivations? First, accept the fact that sin and wrong motivations will always be present. It is part of being human. Second, focus on the right motivation. By focusing on the right motivation, you suppress your wrong motivations and reinforce the right motivations in your thoughts and feelings.

In psychology class, a professor told the story of how he focused on something that he did not want to say in a speech. He rehearsed again and again what he did not want to say. He ended up saying the very thing he did not want to say. He said that which he focused on and rehearsed. This is the reason Christians should focus on the right way to think and behave.

Paul exhorted Christians to think on the right things, saying in Philippians 4:8, "Finally, brethren, whatsoever things are true, whatsoever things are honest, whatsoever things are just, whatsoever things are pure, whatsoever things are lovely, whatsoever things are of good report; if there be any virtue, and if there be any praise, think on these things." By focusing on the right motivation, the right way to think and feel, and the right things to do, you retrain your body of flesh to think and do right.

In Ephesians 4:22–23, Paul says to "… put off concerning the former conversation the old man, which is corrupt according to the deceitful lusts; And be renewed in the spirit of your mind." Renewing the mind involves thinking about doing what is right. It does not remove the presence of sin from the body, but it builds new habits to make it easier to do right. It is never wrong for a Christian to obey God. A Christian cannot justify disobeying God.

If you want to pray right, do right. Being baptized, participating in a local church assembly, reading the Bible, praying, sharing the Gospel with others, training disciples, being honest, being kind, etc., are all part of doing right regardless of feelings. Doing right will always make a Christian stronger and more mature spiritually. It is essential for your prayer life.

HYPOCRISY

Hypocrisy is claiming to be something that you are not. If you are a Christian, it is never hypocritical to say you are a Christian. But it is hypocritical to say that Christ is your Lord yet not live like it. Jesus says in Luke 6:46, "And why call ye me, Lord, Lord, and do not the things which I say."

It is hypocritical to say that Christ is your Lord yet not live like it.

There are two types of hypocrites. There are Christian hypocrites, and there are non-Christian hypocrites. Christian hypocrites live for themselves. They do not serve God. Non-Christian hypocrites live like they serve God.

Christians who call Jesus Christ Lord but do not obey Him are wayward Christians called carnal Christians. Paul used this term in First Corinthians 3:1, "And I, brethren, could not speak unto you as unto spiritual, but as unto carnal, even as unto babes in Christ." Then he said in verse three, "For ye are yet carnal: for whereas there is among you envying, and strife, and divisions, are ye not carnal, and walk as men?" Carnal Christians give Christ and His message a bad reputation. But in spite of their carnality, they are Christians because their inward man is still righteous.

I mentioned the concern some Christians have about always having to feel properly motivated before doing anything for the Lord. The concern is that if they do not feel good about serving the Lord, or if they serve grudgingly, they will be guilty of being falsely motivated. Therefore, they do only that which they feel good about doing. This is wrong thinking. Waiting for the body of flesh to feel good about serving God is living for the flesh, not for God. They should do what is right because God says so, not because they feel like it. The Bible says to obey God. It never says to obey only if you feel like it.

As I mentioned before, the body of flesh is carnal. It is not born again, so it does not willingly submit to obeying God. Oftentimes, it is necessary for Christians to force themselves to do right because it is the right thing to do. This is not hypocrisy. This is obedience. The only time a Christian can truly be a hypocrite is when he does not obey God. Hypocrisy is acting like something you are not. Being a Christian and not acting like it is hypocrisy.

On the other hand, there are the hypocrites who claim to be Christians, but they are not Christians. Jesus said in Matthew 7:21–23, "Not every one that saith unto me, Lord, Lord, shall enter into the kingdom of heaven; but he that doeth the will of my Father which is in heaven. Many will say to me in that day, Lord, Lord, have we not prophesied in thy name? and in thy name have cast out devils? and in thy name done many wonderful works? And then will I profess unto them, I never knew you: depart from me, ye that work iniquity." Doing wonderful works did not make these people hypocrites. It was the claim that they did their works in the name of Christ that made them hypocrites. Christ said He did not know them as His and did not acknowledge that their works were done in His name.

What was their problem? They thought they were Christians. They claimed to be believers. They thought they were doing right. But they were not. They were trying to save themselves their own way, not God's way. They claimed to be doing wonderful works in the name of Christ, but they were really doing these things according to their will, not His.

God makes it clear that salvation must be by grace. To be saved by grace, a person must let God do all the work to save him. This is God's way. The hypocrites mentioned in Matthew 7 claimed they were believers and lived like Christians, but they were not doing God's will. They were doing their own will. They were believers in themselves. They did not believe God's message that salvation was all by grace based on His promise and work. They believed that they were serving God and earning the reward of salvation. They did not believe in being saved God's way. They believed that there was a god to serve, but they did not believe in God's way. They relied on their works as reasons to be accepted by God. This was not God's will. This was disobedience.

The hypocrites mentioned in Matthew 7 claimed they were believers and lived like Christians, but they were not doing God's will. They were doing their own will.

In Matthew 6:5, Jesus cautioned people not to be like the Jewish leaders. He said, "And when thou prayest, thou shalt not be as the hypocrites are: for they love to pray standing in the synagogues and in the corners of the streets, that they may be seen of men. Verily I say unto you, They have their reward." The problem was not with praying in public. God accepted public prayers. The problem was that the hypocrites appeared to be praying to God, but they were not. They prayed to be seen of men. Men saw them, and so the hypocrites received their reward, which was not from God.

Jesus called the Jewish leaders hypocrites because they appeared to know God and to love Him, but they did not. In Matthew 23:27–28, Jesus says, "Woe unto you, scribes and Pharisees, hypocrites! for ye are like unto whited sepulchres, which indeed appear beautiful outward, but are within full of dead men's bones, and of all uncleanness. Even so ye also outwardly appear righteous unto men, but within ye are full of hypocrisy and iniquity." The problem was not that they were living righteously. Their problem was claiming that they were pleasing God and obeying Him. They were not.

Obeying the body of flesh rather than obeying God is the only way a Christian can be a hypocrite. Trusting God and doing right is the only way to avoid being a hypocrite.

THE LOVE FOR RIGHTEOUSNESS

Do you want to enjoy life? Do you want a fulfilling prayer life? Do what is right. Obey God.

The alternative, to sin, results in problems. Lying, cheating, stealing, manipulating others, and hurting others are not conducive to a pleasant and peaceful life. Feelings of jealousy, anger, selfishness, guilt, greed, and hate create internal turmoil and agitation. These things burden the conscience, threaten personal safety, and ruin relationships. A community of sinners creates social disorder and unrest. God's way of doing right is the best way. It produces much better results personally and socially. Living God's way will even make unbelievers' lives better.

Many people are surprised to learn that obeying God boils down to one simple rule. Matthew 22:36–40 is a record of a conversation between a Jewish lawyer and Jesus. It says, "Master, which is the great commandment in the law? Jesus said unto him, Thou shalt love the Lord thy God with all thy heart, and with all thy soul, and with all thy mind. This is the first and great commandment. And the second is like unto it, Thou shalt love thy neighbour as thyself. On these two commandments hang all the law and the prophets."

The first and great command is to love God with all your heart, all your soul, and all your mind. A love for God produces a

To love a righteous God is to love righteousness.

desire to please and obey Him. To love a righteous God is to love righteousness. Loving God also produces a resistance to sin.

Jesus explains the connection between loving God and doing right in John 14:23, saying, "… If a man love me, he will keep my words: and my Father will love him, and we will come unto him, and make our abode with him." To have the presence of God abiding in you is very rewarding. His presence assures you of His love and pleasure. It also provokes a response in you to love Him more.

In John 14:21, Jesus says, "He that hath my commandments, and keepeth them, he it is that loveth me: and he that loveth me shall be loved of my Father, and I will love him, and will manifest myself to him." The manifestation of Christ is an experience that nurtures love for God and satisfies the soul. John 14:21 is a verse that anyone can talk about, but it is only experienced by those who love Him.

Those who love God desire to please Him. Their desire is not out of duty. It is love that produces the desire to please God, even when the task is undesirable to the flesh. Obedience to God is evidence of love for Him. Loving a righteous God means you love to do right. And those who love Him offer prayers that please Him.

MORE THAN LOOKING THE PART

Keeping God's commandments does not *produce* love for God. If it did, legalists such as the Pharisees would have loved Him. The Pharisees obeyed the law and looked righteous, but they were not. They confused looking right with being right. They took pride in obeying the law of God, but they did not love God and did not know God. Jesus said to them in John 8:44, "Ye are of your father the devil, and the lusts of your father ye will do. He was a murderer from the beginning, and abode not in the truth, because there is no truth in him. When he speaketh a lie, he speaketh of his own: for he is a liar, and the father of it." Of course, they protested and said it was not true. But Jesus knew what was in their hearts.

Another good example of how obedience does not produce love for God is the church of Ephesus. Jesus commended them for their works in Revelation 2:2–3, saying, "I know thy works, and thy labour, and thy patience, and how thou canst not bear them which are evil: and thou hast tried them which say they are apostles, and are not, and hast found them liars: And hast borne, and hast patience, and for my name's sake hast laboured, and hast not fainted." The problem with the Ephesian church members was not that they were *doing* anything obviously wrong. Jesus did not scold them for doing good. He encouraged them to continue doing good. But He wanted their love. The problem with them was that they loved doing right more than they loved God. They were sticklers for doctrinal truth and for doing right. However, despite their good works, they left their first love. In fact, they left their first love while serving and obeying God. If doing good works could produce love for God, they would never have left their first love.

Obedience does not produce love. Obedience is the *result* of love, not the *cause* of love. This is the reason it is possible for Satan and his followers to counterfeit the righteous and still be evil. They can act like they are believers with good works and obey God's rules, but they do not love God. If obedience produced love for God, they would love God. All legalists would. Keeping the commandments would be the solution to loving God. But it doesn't work that way. At best, obedience can help maintain the love that already exists.

PRAYING LIKE JESUS

As I mentioned earlier, those who want what God wants have His permission to pray for *whatever* they desire. This permission is not granted to those who do not love Him. It is not granted to those who insist on doing things their own way.

In John 11:22, Martha said to Jesus, "But I know, that even now, whatsoever thou wilt ask of God, God will give it thee." Jesus loved His Father and came to do the will of His Father. Therefore whatever Jesus prayed for was granted. In John 5:19, Jesus says, "... Verily, verily, I say unto you, The Son can do nothing of himself, but what he seeth the Father do: for what things soever he doeth, these also doeth the Son likewise." Jesus wanted the same things His Father wanted, and those who love God have the same desires.

If you love God, you will want what He wants. His goals and purposes will be yours. These desires will guide your prayers, and whatever you pray will be granted. In John 14:13, Jesus says, "And whatsoever ye shall ask in my name, that will I do, that the Father may be glorified in the Son." The prayers of those who love Him are for His glory. These are the prayers Jesus offered.

If you do not love God, you will not pray this way. You will pray selfish prayers. You will pray for selfish goals and for selfish desires. These selfish prayers will not be granted.

LOVING GOD

God grants permission to those who love Him to pray for whatever they want. The prayers of those who love God are the prayers that are offered in Christ's name. When you love God, you will pray for what God desires.

How is it possible to love God this way?

First John 4:19 says, "We love him, because he first loved us." Everything begins with God. God is the origin of all things, even love. He is the fountainhead from which the springs and rivers of love flow. Without God, there is no love.

> *When you love God, you will pray for what God desires.*

The love that we possess in our hearts for God is a love that God initiated. If we have a relationship with Him, He started it. He came to us. He expressed love first.

First John 4:9 explains, "In this was manifested the love of God toward us, because that God sent his only begotten Son into the world, that we might live through him." This verse echoes the familiar words from John 3:16, "For God so loved the world, that he gave his only begotten Son, that whosoever believeth in him should not perish, but have everlasting life." God created humanity as an expression of love. God desired to bless man with His love. But we rejected His love and did things our own way. Now we are suffering the consequences.

Fortunately, God's love for us is so great that He offers forgiveness. We need only to repent. This means that we need to agree that He is right. We need to believe His way is better than our way. At the point of repentance, God grants our request for help and forgiveness. He changes us. We are born again, made right. And now we are capable of loving Him. God's love for us initiates our love for Him.

It is up to us to nurture our love for Him. This means that we must discipline ourselves to do things that will help us overcome the rebellion that is in our bodies of flesh. We will always have to fight against being unloving toward God and toward others. As I already explained, there is no escape from the presence of sin. But we can control it, and we must, if we want to experience God's pleasure with whatever we pray for.

When you love God above all else, His will is your will. His desires are your desires. You want to please Him and live for Him. You no longer fear Him or His will for your life. You pray as Jesus would pray. You pray the prayer that Jesus prayed in the Garden of Gethsemane, "Not my will but thine." You pray in harmony with God's will. And when your desires align with God's desires, your prayers will be granted.

THE MOST IMPORTANT LESSON OF ALL

My life is in God's hands. I trust Him. His plan for my life is the best plan. This is what I pray for. But I know that I am the weak link in His plan for me, so I pray for His help. I am dependent on Him.

I have already shared in this book some of the lessons I learned during my experience with prayer. But the Lord taught me more than just about prayer. I asked the Lord many questions as I read the Bible and was blessed with thoughts and answers that I had not considered before. For example, I asked the Lord to help me understand the experience of Adam and Eve when they sinned. Did they change in some way, and if so, how did they change? How does that change transfer to us? Where do our souls and spirits come from?

The answers to these questions and more flooded my mind. One week, I was writing thoughts down day and night. I felt like

I was traveling through a cave of learning that kept leading to another room of information. I was excited and enjoying the experience. But the thoughts wouldn't stop, and after several days, I was exhausted. I asked the Lord to stop talking to me so I could rest.

The most important lesson we can learn is the answer Jesus gave to the Jewish lawyer mentioned above. In Matthew 22:36–39, the lawyer asked, "Master, which is the great commandment in the law? Jesus said unto him, Thou shalt love the Lord thy God with all thy heart, and with all thy soul, and with all thy mind. This is the first and great commandment. And the second is like unto it, Thou shalt love thy neighbour as thyself. On these two commandments hang all the law and the prophets."

The first and greatest commandment of all commandments is to love God with all your heart, soul, and mind. This means that above all else, the most important thing you can do is to love God first. When God is your first love, then God is the reason for all you do. Nothing is more important. Nothing gets more attention.

God is the Creator of all things. He is the reason for the existence of all things. He is the center of creation. He is the sustainer of creation. He is the reason and the purpose for creation. When God tells us to do something, He is telling us how to function properly in the world He designed. God designed us to love Him. God tells us to love Him with all our heart, soul, and mind because He designed us this way. If we do not love God with all our heart, soul, and mind, then we are not fulfilling our God-given design.

This is like a car designer giving instructions in the owner's manual. People who operate the car as it was designed enjoy their experience of having a car. Those who ignore the instructions ruin their cars. If the car is designed with a gas engine, you should not try to use diesel, kerosene, or water. The same is true with God's instructions. We damage our lives when we ignore His rules.

If you do not understand the value of loving God first as the most important thing you can do, then pray to understand. If you do not love God with all your heart, soul, and mind, then ask God to help you love Him. After salvation, this is the most important prayer request you can make of God because it is the first and greatest of all commandments. You cannot pray right or live right without fulfilling the first and great commandment. Everything you do as a Christian must begin with the first command.

True obedience to God begins with obeying the first and great command. The Apostle Paul said in First Corinthians 13:1–3 that, regardless of all the good works of ministry he did, if he did not have charity (God's love), he was nothing, and his works profited him nothing.

NURTURING YOUR LOVE FOR GOD

If you desire to experience God's pleasure with whatever you pray for, then it is imperative that you love God. Loving God begins and is sustained in your life by asking God to teach you and help you to love Him. If you do not love God or do not love Him as you should, tell Him. He already knows it. So be honest and open about it with Him. To love God as you should, you need to confess your lack of love and ask Him to help you love Him as you should.

As I mentioned before, God has given us three resources to help us grow spiritually and to nurture our love for Him. They are the Word of God, the Spirit of God, and the church of God. How do they help nurture our love for God?

The Word of God is God's message to us. The message is one of love. We learn how God loves us and what He has done for us. We learn of the unimaginable sacrifice He made for us. We learn about His efforts to convince us to turn to Him. As we learn these things and believe Him, we are provoked to respond with appreciation and love. This is one of the ways the Word of God works in us. Paul wrote in First Thessalonians 2:13, "… when ye received the word of God which ye heard of us, ye received it not as the word of men, but as it is in truth, the word of God, which effectually worketh also in you that believe."

God designed us to be responsive. When someone shows kindness to us, we feel appreciative and desire to show kindness in return. When someone is mean to us, we feel inclined to return the same sentiment. This is by design. We are designed to respond to God's love. This is the reason that studying God's Word is a very important part of nurturing our love for Him.

The Holy Spirit is the second resource God gives us. Jesus says in John 14:26, "But the Comforter, which is the Holy Ghost, whom the Father will send in my name, he shall teach you all things, and bring all things to your remembrance, whatsoever I have said unto you." The Spirit of God helps us understand God's word. He reveals God's will to us and guides us.

To benefit from the Spirit, we need to yield to Him. Ephesians 5:18 says, "And be not drunk with wine, wherein is excess; but be filled with the Spirit." To be drunk with wine means to be under the influence of the wine. The admonition in this verse is to be under the influence of the Holy Spirit. When He is our primary influence, we will know God's will and understand how to love Him and how to pray.

The third resource is the church of God. Jesus said in Matthew 16:18, "And I say also unto thee, That thou art Peter, and upon this rock I will build my church; and the gates of hell shall not prevail against it." Jesus built His church during His time on Earth with His followers. Jesus began preparing His church during His ministry to His disciples, but it began its ministry in Jerusalem during Pentecost. Thousands of souls were saved, after which each was baptized, then added to the church, then trained to be disciples of Christ too. This is the purpose of the local church. It is a training center for God's people. It is His embassy in this world. And from Jerusalem, other churches were established throughout Asia Minor, Greece, Rome and around the world. Each local church is a home base for Christians to do God's work His way.

It is Christ's church, not Peter's. Christ built His church to do His work His way. And because He is the ultimate rock-foundation of His church, the gates of hell cannot prevail against it. Anything less than Christ as the foundation would fail in the spiritual battle against evil.

Christians committed to doing God's work God's way do so through a local assembly of believers. Christ did not build His church to be a museum item in the world for people to gawk at and criticize. It was built to be the hub of spiritual activity and ministry to reach the world. Jesus commissioned the first members of His church, telling them in Matthew 28:19–20, "Go ye therefore, and teach all nations, baptizing them in the name of the Father, and of the Son, and of the Holy Ghost: Teaching them to observe all things whatsoever I have commanded you: and, lo, I am with you alway, even unto the end of the world. Amen." This commission shows us that we are to be baptized and to be taught to do everything the disciples did. Acts 2:42 shows the disciples fulfilling the great commission of the church, saying, "And they continued stedfastly in the apostles' doctrine and fellowship, and in breaking of bread, and in prayers."

As with the Word of God and the Spirit of God, the church of God helps to nurture our love for God. Being around others who love God provokes us to want to love God as well. We learn to do so by example, by instruction, and by counsel.

Christians who utilize the three resources of God benefit the most in their experience of living for God. They are committed to doing God's work God's way, and God rewards them for their commitment. Their prayers are granted, and whatever they pray is pleasing to God.

THE SPIRAL CYCLE OF LOVE

Loving God is rewarded with the experience of God's love. Though God loves the world, including the lost for whom He died, the *experience* of God's manifested love and pleasure is reserved only for those who love Him.

In John 14:21, Jesus says, "He that hath my commandments, and keepeth them, he it is that loveth me: and he that loveth me shall be loved of my Father, and I will love him, and will manifest myself to him." The manifestation of love from the Father and from Christ is the reward for loving God. The realness of God's presence, especially of His pleasure and approval, gives you access to a close and personal relationship with your Creator. This is a privileged experience offered to everyone but reserved only for those who love Him. It is this relationship with God that opens the door to knowing His will, gaining insights into His truths, experiencing fulfilling prayers, and enjoying His fellowship with rich, satisfying peace.

As I mentioned before, obedience is not the cause of love. It is the result of love. Obedience will not cause you to love God. However, for Christians obedience is important to nurturing the love they have for God.

In John 14:23, Jesus said, "… If a man love me, he will keep my words: and my Father will love him, and we will come unto him, and make our abode with him." As in John 14:21, Jesus is saying that those who love Him and His Father obey Him. God in turn manifests His love and approval with the realness of His personal presence. This in turn provokes those who love Him to love Him more. God in turn manifests His love for them, and the cycle of expressing love repeats itself.

This cycle of expressing love describes the dynamics of all relationships. When one expresses love, the other responds. This reciprocating love cycle will spiral in increasing love or spiral in decreasing love. It depends on the degree of love expressed or not expressed.

John 21:15–17 records a dialogue between Jesus and Peter that distinguishes between the degrees of love. "So when they had dined, Jesus saith to Simon Peter, Simon, son of Jonas, lovest thou me more than these? He saith unto him, Yea, Lord; thou knowest that I love thee. He saith unto him, Feed my lambs. He saith to him again the second time, Simon, son of Jonas, lovest thou me? He saith unto him, Yea, Lord; thou knowest that I love thee. He saith unto him, Feed my sheep. He saith unto him the third time, Simon, son of Jonas, lovest thou me? Peter was grieved because he said unto him the third time, Lovest thou me? And he said unto him, Lord, thou knowest all things; thou knowest that I love thee. Jesus saith unto him, Feed my sheep."

In this dialogue, Jesus asked Peter three times if he loved Him. The first two times, Jesus used the Greek word *agape*. This is the word used to describe God's sacrificial love for us. Peter responded by saying that he loved Christ, using the word *phileo*. This Greek word refers to a brotherly love. It does not indicate the same degree of sacrificial commitment that *agape* does. Jesus then asked Peter a third time if he loved Him, but He used the Greek word *phileo*. He was willing to accept Peter's *phileo*. Eventually, after he matured, Peter demonstrated *agape* for Christ as a willing martyr for the faith.

Agape comes with time as the spiraling cycle of nurtured love increases. This is the experience of growing spiritually. As one matures spiritually, his love for God increases. And as one's love for God increases, his spiritual maturity increases.

This maturity does not take place in the inward man, which is righteous and already loves God perfectly. Rather, it is the training of the outward man to love God. The body struggles with carnal passions of sin, anger, hate, jealousy, and greed. So love for God in the outward man requires that we nurture love for God. This is the reason God gives us the three resources. We must use these resources to nurture our love for God, obey Him, and pray for His help.

PRAYING TO LOVE GOD AND TO KNOW HIS WILL

Having a love for God means more than having a personal relationship with God and knowledge of God's desires, His will, and His preferences. It means desiring what God desires. Christians who love God are given permission to pray for whatever they want because they pray for God's will to be done. What would Jesus pray for? Everything His Father would want.

Christians who love God are given permission to pray for whatever they want because they pray for God's will to be done.

Since Jesus was divinely perfect in all His ways and wanted only His Father's will, why did the Father not grant Jesus' request to be delivered from death? And why was Paul not granted his request for removing an annoyance out of his life? Why were martyrs not granted their requests for deliverance from death? These were servants of God.

Jesus prayed to His Father in John 12:27, "Now is my soul troubled; and what shall I say? Father, save me from this hour: but for this cause came I unto this hour." This shows that Jesus dreaded the experience of eternal death He was about to endure. Nonetheless, He was committed to doing it out of love for us. He asked His Father to save Him from the experience yet was willing to be told no. Why? Because Jesus willingly committed Himself to making the sacrifice. The Father did not have to tell Him no. Jesus already knew the answer. Jesus already knew that there was no other way to save the souls of humanity. He dreaded the experience of eternal condemnation, but He did it because of love.

Likewise, Paul and many martyrs accepted God's answers to their prayers because their first desire was for God's will to be done. I will address this in more detail later in the book. But the point here is that having permission to ask for whatever you want does not mean that you will be granted your request. And being denied your request does not necessarily mean that you do not love God.

Focus on the first and great commandment to love God. As your love for Him grows, your wants will align with His. Your prayer requests will be guided by His purpose. You will desire that His will be done above all else. And whatever you pray will be for the purpose of fulfilling God's will.

PRAYING FOR HEALTH, WEALTH, AND LIFE

For many people, the idea of praying for whatever they want conjures up the image of having a genie in a lamp to grant their every wish to fulfill their lusts of greed, selfishness, and vengeance. Obviously, this is not how it works.

The winning of souls to Christ is what guides God's answers.

However, as one who loves God, you are granted permission to pray for anything. As one who loves God, your prayers for health, wealth, and life are not rooted in sin and lust. Your prayers will be guided by a concern for furthering your ministry and the ministry of others to win souls to Christ and to train others to do likewise. The winning of souls to Christ is what guides God's answers.

If you are ill, ask God to heal you. If your lack of funds hinders your ministry, ask Him to supply your needs. If you are facing the prospect of dying, ask God to spare your life so that you can continue your ministry longer.

The Apostle Paul expresses in Philippians 1:21–26 the proper attitude about life and death. He writes, "For to me to live [is] Christ, and to die [is] gain. But if I live in the flesh, this [is] the fruit of my labour: yet what I shall choose I wot not. For I am in a strait betwixt two, having a desire to depart, and to be with Christ; which is far better: Nevertheless to abide in the flesh [is] more needful for you. And having this confidence, I know that I shall abide and continue with you all for your furtherance and joy of faith; That your rejoicing may be more abundant in Jesus Christ for me by my coming to you again." Paul could pray that God's will be done, whether it be to go to heaven sooner or later. Paul could accept God's answer either way. Why? Because he knew God's answer would be the best answer. God's answer would ultimately be the granting of Paul's prayer.

Like Paul, I was assured by God that I had permission to pray for my life. He extended my life. I have served Him and have been engaged in ministry to fulfill His purpose. For how much longer? I do not know. Everyone dies at some point.

The important thing is to rest in God's love. Love Him, pray for whatever you want, and serve Him to the best of your ability. This is the right way to pray.

GREAT INSIGHTS TO REMEMBER

1. God's way is always the right way.
2. You can ask whatever you want, but you will receive only that which does not violate God's will.

3. Until you can pray "Not my will, but Yours be done," you will not know the experience of mountain-moving prayers.

4. When your desires are God's desires, then anything you pray for will be granted.

5. It makes no sense to return to sin after asking God to deliver you.

6. To pray the right way, you need to know by faith what you can pray for. You need to believe that you can pray for it. And you must offer your prayers in righteousness.

7. Being right requires being saved. This is God's work. Doing right is living right. This is your work.

8. Motivation because of a sense of responsibility is the right motivation.

9. It is never wrong for a Christian to obey God. Everything you do for God is acceptable to Him.

10. With the righteousness of the new, inward man, the aid of the Holy Spirit, fellowship with God, and His resources to help us, we can live the life of victory over sin. We can obey God and enjoy the life of blessings that He intended for us.

11. There are two criteria required to pray right. First, to pray right, you must be right. Second, to pray right, you must live right.

12. It is always right to do right. It is never wrong to do right, and it is never right to do wrong.

13. The privilege to experience a personal relationship with God is offered to everyone but reserved only for those who love Him.

3
PRAYERS BECAUSE OF REVELATION

Let it be known this day that thou art God in Israel,
and that I am thy servant, and that I have done
all these things at thy word.
—First Kings 18:36

Prayers because of revelation are one of four types of prayers. They are guaranteed to be granted if we believe and pray. They are prayers that God tells us to pray, so they are backed by His will and power. Nothing can prevent the prayers that are offered up because of revelation.

In the Old Testament, Elijah the prophet prayed a prayer because of revelation at Mt. Carmel during his contest with the priests of Baal. In First Kings 18:36, Elijah says, "… LORD God of Abraham, Isaac, and of Israel, let it be known this day that thou art God in Israel, and that I am thy servant, and that I have done all these things at thy word." Elijah did not make this request on his initiative. He was praying for fire to come down from heaven because God had revealed to him what to ask for. This is what makes the *prayers because of revelation* different from the *prayers for desires* and *for revelation*.

These are prayers that *will* move mountains and *will* make the impossible happen because God has revealed that this is what He wants. There is no more sure prayer than a *prayer because of revelation*. All we need to do is recognize what God wants us to pray for, believe it, and pray for it. Is this difficult to do? Not at all.

GOD'S WILL REVEALED

God reveals His will in three ways: by His Spirit through faith, in His written Word (the Bible), and by godly counsel. Revelation simply means to make something known. Revelation by His Spirit is very specific and individualized. Revelation in His written Word is general and applies to everyone or identified groups of people. Revelation by godly counsel confirms what God has made known personally by the Holy Spirit and/or generally through His Word.

> *God reveals His will in three ways: by His Spirit through faith, in His written Word, and by godly counsel.*

By His Spirit through faith. Knowledge of what to pray for by faith comes from the Holy Spirit. He personalizes His revealed instruction directly from God to each of us individually. This is how Elijah knew that he should pray for fire to come out of heaven to consume the sacrifice. This was not a prayer he initiated. Elijah prayed because God told him what to pray for. Prayers because of revelation by the Spirit are not common in the Bible.

In the Bible. The Bible gives general revelation that applies to designated groups of people or to all people. For example, Paul writes in Colossians 4:12, "Epaphras, who is one of you, a servant of Christ, saluteth you, always labouring fervently for you in prayers, that ye may stand perfect and complete in all the will of God." Epaphras offered, in this case, intercessory prayers because of revelation. His prayer for others to "stand perfect and complete in all the will of God" is a prayer that should be made for all Christians. Second Timothy 3:16–17 says, "All scripture is given by inspiration of God, and is profitable for doctrine, for reproof, for correction, for instruction in righteousness: That the man of God may be perfect, throughly furnished unto all good works." With this in mind, we know that we can pray for ourselves and for others to be "perfect, throughly furnished unto all good works." To be *perfect* means to be complete or mature as in being a good representation of Christ. Prayers because of revelation by the Word of God are very common.

As disciples, we follow Christ's example of doing good. The better we follow His example, the better we represent Him. This is God's will, and we can pray for this to happen in every Christian's life. This is a prayer that He will always grant. God will do His part, but we must be willing to do our part by obeying Him. If we believe and pray for spiritual maturity, it is guaranteed to happen. It is the will of God.

By godly counsel. Godly counsel personalizes God's will with the aid of the Holy Spirit, God's Word, and experience. Mature, veteran Christian men and women who have experience with prayer, with discerning God's will, and with serving Christ can provide valuable spiritual guidance.

Experience with discerning God's will over time builds confidence in recognizing the voice of God.

PRAYERS REVEALED BY THE HOLY SPIRIT

Revelations from the Holy Spirit are revelations from God *personalized* for our lives. In my case, after two weeks of praying for revelation, God revealed to me that I had His permission to pray for my life. There was no written message to me in the Bible, and there were no counselors at this point telling me that God planned to heal me. This was a message directly from God to me. It was personalized for me. God does not heal everyone all the time.

How could I be so certain that God was talking to me? First of all, I had some experience discerning God's will. This was not the first time God had talked to me. Experience with discerning God's will over time builds confidence in recognizing the voice of God. Nonetheless, it is important to test whether a thought is from God. First John 4:1–3 cautions, "… believe not every spirit, but try the spirits whether they are of God: because many false prophets are gone out into the world. Hereby know ye the Spirit of God: Every spirit that confesseth that Jesus Christ is come in the flesh is of God: And every spirit that confesseth not that Jesus Christ is come in the flesh is not of God."

Second, in addition to having experience, it is necessary to apply the truth test to determine whether a thought is from God. Jesus said in John 16:13, "Howbeit when he, the Spirit of truth, is come, he will guide you into all truth: for he shall not speak of himself; but whatsoever he shall hear, that shall he speak: and he will shew you things to come." Whatever the Spirit of God says will always be in unity with the message from God the Father and from Christ. There is only one truth. If you have a thought that is contrary to the truth of God revealed in His Word, the Bible, you should reexamine the thought because something is not right.

In my case, there was not a doctrinal conflict. The Bible speaks of healings by Jesus, by His disciples, and by others. In fact, praying to be healed is encouraged (James 5:14). So being healed was not contrary to God's Word. Furthermore, I did not detect any contrary spiritual presence or force denying that Christ is Lord, God, and Savior. I was very much at peace with God, and I felt a release from the uncertainty that had motivated me to *pray for revelation*.

A third way to test whether a thought is from God is to seek confirmation through godly counsel. My pastor and others in my church confirmed that God wanted to heal me. In the Bible, the calling of Barnabus and Saul as missionaries was confirmed by the church of Antioch due to direct revelation from the Holy Spirit. Acts 13:2 describes the church leaders, saying, "As they ministered to the Lord, and fasted, the Holy Ghost said, Separate me Barnabas and Saul for the work whereunto I have called them." The church was used by God to publicly authorize and legitimize the sending of Barnabas and Saul, but it was the Spirit of God who is credited with sending Barnabas and Saul as indicated by Acts 13:4, "So they, being sent forth by the Holy Ghost, departed unto Seleucia; and from thence they sailed to Cyprus." The *prayers because of revelation* for the approval and sending of Barnabas and Saul were guaranteed to be honored by God.

A fourth helpful test is to identify a compelling reason. Is what you desire obviously beneficial to accomplishing God's purpose of winning souls? For me, I had compelling reasons to pray for my healing, including being around for my family and for my ministry to others.

Any one of these tests individually may have left room to question if God were really telling me that I could pray for my healing. But together, these four things served to confirm God's message to me and gave me confidence that God was revealing His answer to me. At that point, I was ready to pray with the confidence that comes with *prayers because of revelation*.

UNSOLICITED REVELATION

I asked God to reveal to me what He wanted me to pray for. Then because I received His answer, I prayed. But occasionally, God reveals His will without a request. Elijah is a good example, and Moses is a good example. Not many in the Bible are selected for unsolicited revelations, so this is not something that is common.

The well-known Bible story of Moses challenging Pharaoh involved prayers because of revelation. God revealed to Moses what to say to Pharaoh and what to pray. In Exodus 7:2, God told Moses directly, "Thou shalt speak all that I command thee: and Aaron thy brother shall speak unto Pharaoh, that he send the children of Israel out of his land." Exodus 7:6 says, "And Moses and Aaron did as the LORD commanded them, so did they." And so the miracles of ten plagues on Egypt took place because Moses prayed according to the revelation he received from God. For example, Exodus 8:16 says, "And the LORD said unto Moses, Say unto Aaron, Stretch out thy rod, and smite the dust of the land, that it may become lice throughout all the land of Egypt." In the case of the plagues, God told Moses what to pray and when to pray it.

On another occasion, Elijah prayed because of revelation. Besides praying for fire to come out of heaven to consume the sacrifice on Mount Carmel, Elijah also prayed because of revelation from God to stop the rain for three years and then to cause it to rain again. First Kings 18:1 says, "And it came to pass after many days, that the word of the LORD came to Elijah in the third year, saying, Go, shew thyself unto Ahab; and I will send rain upon the earth." God was telling Elijah what His plan was and what to pray for. Elijah believed, prayed, and it was so.

Another example of revelation by the Spirit is recorded in Second Chronicles 7:14. The Lord told Solomon, "If my people, which are called by my name, shall humble themselves, and pray, and seek my face, and turn from their wicked ways; then will I hear from heaven, and will forgive their sin, and will heal their land." This was a revelation from God to Solomon and Israel telling them what to do and what to pray for if they were ever cursed.

The recipients of unsolicited revelations from God need only to believe and pray. It might at first appear that only the most godly would receive such revelations. But there are exceptions.

For example, God revealed to Israel to pray for deliverance when they were under judgment. If they had believed and prayed, they would have been delivered. But they did not believe. They rejected God's invitation. Jesus says of them in Luke 13:34, "O Jerusalem, Jerusalem, which killest the prophets, and stonest them that are sent unto thee; how often would I have gathered thy children together, as a hen doth gather her brood under her wings, and ye would not!"

Another example of unsolicited revelation is when God reveals His will to the lost. His will is to save them. Jesus gives the universal invitation in Matthew 11:28, saying, "Come unto me, all ye that labour and are heavy laden, and I will give you rest." In John 16:7–11, Jesus expresses how the Holy Spirit (the Comforter) reveals the need for salvation, saying, "... he will reprove the world of sin, and of righteousness, and of judgment."

God reveals His will to the lost by His Spirit, in His written Word, and by His witnesses.

Second Peter 3:9 expresses the desire of God written in His Word, saying, He "... is longsuffering to us-ward, not willing that any should perish, but that all should come to repentance." And like the prophets since the foundation of the world, Christians continue to proclaim and reveal the good news of God's salvation message. In Luke 1:70, an angel declares that God revealed His promise of salvation, saying, "As he spake by the mouth of his holy prophets, which have been since the world began" (cf. Titus 1:2).

Tragically, most reject His word and do not believe. In Matthew 22:14, Jesus says, "For many are called, but few are chosen." God wants to save everyone. His call and invitation is to everyone. This is His will. But He will not force His will on anyone. He reveals His will and then waits for souls to believe Him. He saves the believers. Only believers are chosen to receive His gift of salvation. Believing is the criterion God requires. This is their acceptance of God's will. And the moment one believes, God grants the request for salvation. This is a guaranteed prayer because of revelation.

PRAYERS REVEALED IN THE BIBLE

Prayers because of revelation by God's written Word are abundant. This is the easiest way to discover what to pray for. Having God's will written in a book eliminates the uncertainty of hearing God's thoughts in your mind or of relying on others to tell you what God's will is. Having it written down also allows for objective discovery that can be verified by others.

Unlike revelation from the Spirit, revelation from the written Word of God is not tailored to just one person at a time. It is God's will expressed generally, and it usually applies to everyone or to named groups. For example, Second Corinthians 5:17–20 says, "Therefore if any man be in Christ, he is a new creature: old things are passed away; behold, all things are become new. And all things are of God, who hath reconciled us to himself by Jesus Christ, and hath given to us the ministry of reconciliation; To wit, that God was in Christ, reconciling the world unto himself, not imputing their trespasses unto them; and hath committed unto us the word of reconciliation. Now then we are ambassadors for Christ, as though God did beseech you by us: we pray you in Christ's stead, be ye reconciled to God."

This passage shows that God changes Christians and gives them new responsibilities. I have already explained how He changes believers by the miracle of new birth to give them a new nature spiritually. As a group, Christians are also given a new purpose in life to represent God as ambassadors with the ministry of reconciliation. This involves sharing the Gospel news of God to explain to others how to experience salvation. Christians who pray to fulfill this responsibility can expect their prayers to be answered, especially prayers for their development of skills to share the Gospel message more effectively with others. Based on this written revelation, Christians are guaranteed that their sincere prayers to be effective in their ministries as representatives for Christ will be granted.

There are many revelations in the Bible about things to pray for. Jesus says in Luke 10:2, "... The harvest truly is great, but the labourers are few: pray ye therefore the Lord of the harvest, that he would send forth labourers into his harvest." God wants you to pray for more believers to participate in reaching the world with His Gospel message.

In Matthew 6:9–15, Jesus says that we should pray for His kingdom to come, for His will to be done on earth as it is done in heaven, for our daily needs, for forgiveness, for protection from temptation, and for deliverance from evil. First Timothy 2:1–3 tells us that we should pray for all men, for all that are in authority, and for a quiet and peaceable life because these things are "good and acceptable in the sight of God our Saviour."

Likewise, the prayer for salvation is guaranteed in His Word. God's will is revealed in Romans 10:13, which says, "For whosoever shall call upon the name of the Lord shall be saved." Salvation takes place by simply believing God. Because of believing, you are saved. God's message to be believed is that Jesus is God, that He is the Lord and Savior for you, and that His promise is to save you by grace and not as a reward for your efforts. God guarantees that He will save anyone who believes Him. In John 11:25, Jesus said to Martha, "I am the resurrection, and the life: he that believeth in me, though he were dead, yet shall he live: And whosoever liveth and believeth in me shall never die. Believest thou this?" Salvation prayers with scripted words do not save people. There is no formula to say and no deeds to do in order to be saved. Telling others that you believe in God will not save you. You simply believe in Jesus Christ. This is how you personally respond and call on God. This is the revealed message of God in His Word.

Included in the category of *prayers because of revelation* are the *prayers for revelation*. Prayers for revelation are offered *because* of revelation from God encouraging believers to pray and make requests of Him. James 1:5 says, "If any of you lack wisdom, let him ask of God, that giveth to all men liberally, and upbraideth not; and it shall be given him." If you do not know what to pray for, you should ask God. This is what I did. I did not presume that God would heal me. I wanted to know His will so that I could pray fully confident in His will. I did not want to pray against what His will was. I was willing to accept His will whatever it was.

Jesus says in Matthew 7:7, "Ask, and it shall be given you; seek, and ye shall find; knock, and it shall be opened unto you." When you ask God to show you what to pray for, He will show you, if that truly is your desire, whether it be for revelation about the person to marry, the house to buy or rent, or the church He wants you in. You can pray to know what to pray for because it is God's will that you have the wisdom to know what to pray for.

If you are not interested in praying for God's written revealed will, then you are not really interested in God's will being done.

Do these verses help you understand what to pray for? They are easy to find, and God's will is stated plainly. Having these prayers written down takes the mystery out of knowing what to pray for. But more importantly, these verses *are* the written will of God. These revelations show you what God wants you to pray for. If you are not interested in praying for God's written revealed will, then you are not really interested in God's will being done. If this be the case, then there is no reason to expect that God will show you His will by His Spirit.

PRAYERS REVEALED BY COUNSEL

In addition to having the written revelation of God's will, the counsel of those who serve God can help reveal to us what to pray for. They reveal God's will by explaining what God reveals in the Bible, and they confirm God's will as they are directed by the Holy Spirit. They also give advice based on their experiences of discerning the will of God.

As mentioned earlier, Acts 13:2 says of the church leaders at Antioch, "As they ministered to the Lord, and fasted, the Holy Ghost said, Separate me Barnabas and Saul for the work whereunto I have called them." God's Spirit gave the church leaders personalized instruction to confirm the calling of Barnabas and Saul.

The Holy Spirit called Barnabas and Saul but used their church leaders to confirm the Spirit's calling. God does not require you to rely on others to know His will. But He does use others to confirm and legitimize what God is already telling you. This is one way God protects the legitimacy of His work and provides safety for those who serve Him.

There should be unanimity among those giving counsel about a particular matter when a definitive answer from God is expected.

A lack of consensus among counselors may be due to a misunderstanding of the counsel of God. Another reason for conflicting counsel may be that God has not given a definitive answer. It is important at this point to recognize this *silent answer* and interpret it correctly. Does this silent answer mean to wait for a definite answer? Does it mean that God is leaving the choice up to the individual? Or is there sin among the counselors or distraction by Satan creating confusion? In any case, misunderstanding God's counsel, silent answers, or distractions could explain the lack of consensus among counselors.

For church decisions, it is up to the pastor to make the final determination. Church members are responsible to honor the pastor's decision. A decision made is better than indecisiveness and confusion. And unity among church counselors is better than division and confusion. James 3:16 warns, "For where envying and strife is, there is confusion and every evil work." Do not give the Devil opportunity to harm the church by rebelling against the pastor. Pray, participate in offering suggestions, and then unite in letting God direct the pastor.

When there is conflicting counsel given for your personal decisions, be cautious. God does not give different counsel from person to person, nor does He give counsel that is contrary to His Word. There is either an evil influence at work, or a silent answer from God giving you permission to make the decision. In either case, the choice is up to you.

Counsel comes from many sources. It is recognized in churches that the pastor and his staff are the primary sources of Biblical counsel. But husbands and wives counsel each other. Friends counsel each other. Even strangers share their counsel with others. It is important to identify the value and spiritual expertise of each of the different sources of counsel.

For ministry decisions, God gives you a church with a pastor and ordained leaders. This is the precedence set in the early church. Acts 14:23 says, "And when they had ordained them elders in every church, and had prayed with fasting, they commended them to the Lord, on whom they believed." Paul explains in Philippians 3:17 the importance of identifying leaders in your church, saying, "Brethren, be followers together of me, and mark them which walk so as ye have us for an ensample."

Godly counselors rely on the Holy Spirit and personal experience to counsel and to advise on personal application of God's Word. This lends safety to making wise and right choices. By God's design of the church, godly pastors and church leaders are carefully selected by the Spirit of God and the church members to provide the leadership of example and counsel.

God expects us to seek godly counsel from church leaders. Ephesians 4:11–12 says, "And he gave some, apostles; and some, prophets; and some, evangelists; and some, pastors and teachers; For the perfecting of the saints, for the work of the ministry, for the edifying of the body of Christ." God gives us counselors in His church to help us. It is our personal responsibility to seek that godly counsel. Proverbs 11:14 says, "Where no counsel is, the people fall: but in the multitude of counsellors there is safety."

Regardless of the advice and counsel given, you are the one who ultimately makes the choice of what you will do.

It is important to recognize what kind of counsel to avoid. Psalm 1:1 says, "Blessed is the man that walketh not in the counsel of the ungodly, nor standeth in the way of sinners, nor sitteth in the seat of the scornful." Furthermore, if you think that you have no need of counsel from others, you may be your own worst enemy. Proverbs 12:15 warns, "The way of a fool is right in his own eyes: but he that hearkeneth unto counsel is wise."

Ultimately, you are responsible for the decisions you make. Regardless of the advice and counsel given, you are the one who decides what you will do. Some choose to let others make the decisions for them. This is a personal choice, and sometimes, to rely on those who are more informed could be the best thing. But it is still your choice to rely on someone else's decision. If the counsel from others was not best for you, the responsibility and consequences are still yours to own.

LEAD US NOT INTO TEMPTATION

In Matthew 6:13, Jesus instructed His disciples to pray "And lead us not into temptation, but deliver us from evil...." This is a revealed prayer request. You can ask to be delivered from evil, and it will come to pass, if not now, later. As I mentioned before, suffering is a part of living in a world of sin. Good and bad things happen to all people. Jesus, while in this world of sin, was opposed, hated, and attacked. Those who follow Him should expect the same.

Jesus says in John 15:19–20, "If ye were of the world, the world would love his own: but because ye are not of the world, but I have chosen you out of the world, therefore the world hateth you. Remember the word that I said unto you, The servant is not greater than his lord. If they have persecuted me, they will also persecute you; if they have kept my saying, they will keep yours also." It is ironic that Jesus brought a message of hope, love, and grace but was hated and shown no grace. We need to pray to be delivered from this evil as well.

Jesus told us to pray to our Father in heaven, asking to not be led into temptation but to be delivered from evil. Of course, we all want to avoid pain and suffering, but they are part of living in a world of sin. Suffering and death are the consequences of sin. Some suffer more than others, but everyone suffers at some time in life. There is no escape from sin; therefore, there is no escape from suffering and death.

Before sin entered the world, there was no suffering or death. But once sin was introduced in the world, suffering and death began. This suffering will continue until Christ judges all sinners and creates a new heaven and earth where there will be no sin.

Obviously, the disciples suffered due to hardships, deprivations, and martyrdom. Paul the Apostle recounts his experiences in Second Corinthians 11:24–27, saying, "Of the Jews five times received I forty stripes save one. Thrice was I beaten with rods, once was I stoned, thrice I suffered shipwreck, a night and a day I have been in the deep; In journeyings often, in perils of waters, in perils of robbers, in perils by mine own countrymen, in perils by the heathen, in perils in the city, in perils in the wilderness, in perils in the sea, in perils among false brethren; In weariness and painfulness, in watchings often, in hunger and thirst, in fastings often, in cold and nakedness."

Did Paul and the other disciples disobey God and not pray to be delivered from temptation and evil? Of course not. Paul asked for prayer in Second Thessalonians 3:2, "… that we may be delivered from unreasonable and wicked men: for all men have not faith." And in Romans 15:30–31, Paul writes, "Now I beseech you, brethren, for the Lord Jesus Christ's sake, and for the love of the Spirit, that ye strive together with me in your prayers to God for me; That I may be delivered from them that do not believe in Judaea; and that my service which I have for Jerusalem may be accepted of the saints."

Despite praying for deliverance, Paul suffered anyway. And so did the other disciples. Many Christians have prayed for deliverance and yet suffered. Why are so many Christians not delivered, especially since Jesus told us to pray that we not be led into temptation and to pray for deliverance from evil?

Every answer from God fulfills His purpose of winning souls now and into the future. He sees the chain of events that leads to the maximum number of souls saved. For some, this includes suffering at the moment. Nonetheless, eventually all prayers by believers for deliverance from evil will be answered. Paul and the other disciples are enjoying eternal deliverance right now. Galatians 1:4 explains the hope we have of deliverance, saying that Christ "... gave himself for our sins, that he might deliver us from this present evil world, according to the will of God and our Father."

Some complain that God should not allow sin and suffering. Some wonder what good it does to pray if God allows suffering. Unlike us, God sees the big picture. Like looking at a chessboard, He knows what move to make even though the pieces are thinking only of themselves. In Revelation 6, He tells the martyrs in heaven crying out for vengeance to wait until their fellow-servants are killed even as they were. God's plan includes suffering. He does not desire any to suffer, but it is part of the experience of living in a world of sin.

Suffering comes with living in a world filled with sin. Everyone suffers in some way, some more than others. For most, God allows the course of life to unfold with the good and the bad. As we share in the experiences that are common in life, we as believers experience the additional blessings of God's strength and comfort as we walk through this life. He blesses those who serve Him with peace. If He does not deliver us from evil at the moment, He delivers us with strength to endure the evil at the moment.

In First Corinthians 10:13, Paul writes, "There hath no temptation taken you but such as is common to man: but God is faithful, who will not suffer you to be tempted above that ye are able; but will with the temptation also make a way to escape, that ye may be able

The prayer for deliverance is a prayer request of believers that will always be answered, guaranteed.

to bear it." Paul wrote in Philippians 4:7 of having supernatural peace, saying, "And the peace of God, which passeth all understanding, shall keep your hearts and minds through Christ Jesus." For some, deliverance is immediate. For others, deliverance is postponed. But the prayer for deliverance is a prayer request of believers that will always be answered, guaranteed. Paul was not discouraged by the delay. He was faithful in spite of the suffering he endured. James 1:2 explains how to think about suffering, saying, "My brethren, count it all joy when ye fall into divers temptations." This attitude is possible when one trusts God to do that which is best for fulfilling His primary objective of winning souls.

Looking at the big picture, all suffering will be eliminated with the elimination of sin. And the current sufferings in this world pale compared to the eternal tranquility and blessings to come. In Romans 8:18, Paul says, "For I reckon that the sufferings of this present time [are] not worthy [to be compared] with the glory which shall be revealed in us." God sympathizes with our suffering. He plans to eliminate it permanently. But He is working out the best plan possible to save as many souls as possible.

Though God desires that no one suffer, many of His children, including His disciples, have been martyred. But the day is coming when their prayer for vengeance will be answered. The day is coming when believers will never be tempted again; they will never face death again; and they will never face evil again. That day is coming when God sets up His kingdom of heaven. Until then, we must wait patiently as He said to the martyrs in Revelation 6:11, "… that they should rest yet for a little season, until their fellow servants also and their brethren, that should be killed as they were, should be fulfilled."

Because suffering is part of living in a sin-filled world, suffering is included in God's will. In other words, preventing suffering is not always God's will. God designed this world. It is doing exactly what He designed it to do. God is not obligated in any way to remove suffering out of our lives or out of the world. If we sin, suffering, by design, is a predictable consequence. A guilty conscience is part of our design. Suffering causes us to look for a solution. For those who recognize that sin brings sorrow and that sorrow brings a search for solutions, there is recognition of the value of suffering in a world of sin. Ultimately, any rational person will recognize that seeking God's help is required to escape sin and its consequences. His plan is to save as many souls as possible, and everything He does is for that purpose. This is the reason suffering is included in the experience of living.

MY MOUNTAIN

God reveals in His Word and by His Spirit through faith that it is possible to pray prayers that move mountains. I prayed to understand these kinds of prayers, and God answered my prayer by giving me a mountain to move. When I was diagnosed with cancer, I did not know how I should pray, so I asked God to show me if I should pray for my life. I believed that He would grant this request for revelation of His will. Within two weeks, God revealed to me that I had His permission to pray for my life. My *prayer for revelation* resulted in praying for healing *because of revelation*.

God answered my prayer to know what to pray for. The answer I received was permission to pray for healing. Permission was granted because He was willing to heal me. I knew this. If there were no chance of the request being granted, then God would have answered my prayer with a definite no. But the answer of granting permission to ask for healing indicated that my healing would require that I believe and pray. I was responsible for having my prayer granted. I needed to believe that God desired to grant my request and would do so.

Everyone should pray for revelation of God's will. He wants

you to know His plan for your life. Read your Bible, pray for the Spirit to guide you, and seek counsel from godly believers. Knowing what you should pray for will give you great confidence in your prayer life.

GREAT INSIGHTS TO REMEMBER

1. Prayers because of revelation are guaranteed to be granted if we believe and pray.

2. Prayers because of revelation will make the impossible happen because they are prayers that God wants to answer.

3. God reveals His will by means of His Spirit through faith, in His written Word, and by godly counsel.

4. Revelation by the Holy Spirit through faith is personalized revelation.

5. Revelation from the Word of God is general revelation.

6. Revelation by godly counsel personalizes God's will with the aid of the Holy Spirit, God's Word, and experience.

7. Granted prayers for revelation will lead to prayers because of revelation.

8. The tests of truth for thoughts from God are:

   1) Experience

   2) Consistency with the Word of God

   3) Confirmation from counselors

   4) Compelling reasons to fulfill God's work

9. God gives everyone unsolicited revelation for salvation.

10. A lack of consensus among counselors may be due to misunderstanding the counsel of God.

11. Where no counsel is, the people fall, but in the multitude of counselors there is safety.

12. You are responsible for the decisions you make.

13. Prayers because of revelation will always be granted to believers sooner or later.

4
PRAYERS OF INTERCESSION

Moreover as for me, God forbid that I should
sin against the LORD in ceasing to pray for you:
but I will teach you the good and the right way.
—First Samuel 12:23

During my time of coping with chemotherapy treatments, many people sent cards and emails to me to let me know they were praying for me and wishing me well. Some called me on the phone. These expressions of love and concern put a smile on my face just to know that someone was thinking about me. Most of the notes said they were praying for my comfort and recovery. I cannot express how grateful I was to see those words, especially during the most difficult times. I was glad to hear that people cared enough to pray for me.

Prayers offered on behalf of someone else are called *intercessory prayers*. These are a blessing to all involved. Those prayed for are benefited, and those who offer prayers on behalf of the beneficiaries are blessed as well.

Paul wrote in Second Corinthians 1:11, "Ye also helping together by prayer for us, that for the gift [bestowed] upon us by the means of many persons thanks may be given by many on our behalf." Paul encouraged and thanked the Corinthians for their prayers. Their prayers were a help to Paul and to those with him as they ministered to others. God's gift bestowed on Paul to minister was credited to the many who offered prayers on his behalf. As a result, many were blessed by Paul's ministry. Those who prayed were blessed with being credited for helping his ministry to others, and those receiving the ministry were blessed.

Many will be blessed by God because they believed and cared enough to pray for me. He answered their prayers, and they are credited by God for helping me. As a result of my recovery, I have taught, counseled, and helped hundreds of people. Souls have been saved and disciples trained. Every person who prayed for my recovery shares in the blessings and ministries that have taken place since my recovery. The many people benefiting from the message of this book are blessed because God answered the prayers for my healing.

Every person who prayed for my recovery shares in the blessings and ministries that have taken place since my recovery.

BLESSINGS FOR ALL

Intercessory prayers are a way of multiplying blessings to many people. There is no limit to the number of people who can pray for others and who can share in the answers to those prayers. God gives unlimited opportunities for an unlimited number of people to share in the prayers answered. The saving of a soul, the discipleship of a soul, the recovery from an illness, the funding for a mission project, and much more are credited to every person who prays.

Intercessory prayer has been a big part of church ministry since its beginning. Acts 12:5 says of the disciples during Peter's imprisonment, "Peter therefore was kept in prison: but prayer was made without ceasing of the church unto God for him." Everyone who prayed for Peter's release and safety were a part of that granted prayer.

The larger the prayer group, the greater the number of people who will be blessed when prayers are granted. Can you imagine being on a prayer team that prays for people all over the world? God makes it possible for you to share in every ministry that is occurring in the world. This is truly inspiring. It makes me want to pray more often for more. How about you?

I tell folks that when we pray for missionaries, we are contributing to the success of those ministries. Every Wednesday evening, we meet in prayer teams throughout our church. And during the week, prayer letters are sent to and shared with members of our church. Everyone who prays becomes a participant in the ministries they pray for. There is no limit placed on the number of prayers that can be offered or on the number of people who can pray.

GOD REQUIRES INTERCESSORY PRAYER

Intercessory prayers are expected of Christians. Whether or not we understand the purpose of prayer or the significance of intercession, God expects us to pray for others.

God commanded the priests to pray for Israel's peace. Failure to pray for God's blessings on Israel would have been disobedience. God revealed to Moses that he should tell Aaron, the high priest, to bless Israel. In Numbers 6:23–26, God says to Moses, "Speak unto Aaron and unto his sons, saying, On this wise ye shall bless the children of Israel, saying unto them, The LORD bless thee, and keep thee: The LORD make his face shine upon thee, and be gracious unto thee: The LORD lift up his countenance upon thee, and give thee peace." This prayer of blessings for Israel expresses what God desired for Israel. He wanted Aaron to pray for Israel's blessings in accordance to His desires. The well-known judge of Israel, Samuel, indicated that it would be sin if he did not pray for others, saying in First Samuel 12:23, "Moreover as for me, God forbid that I should sin against the LORD in ceasing to pray for you ...." King David prayed for Israel and admonished others to do so in Psalm 122:6, saying, "Pray for the peace of Jerusalem: they shall prosper that love thee." God expects us to pray for the peace of Israel.

Jesus offered intercessory prayers for others and still does. Hebrews 7:25 says of Jesus, "Wherefore he is able also to save them to the uttermost that come unto God by him, seeing he ever liveth to make intercession for them." Though we are not substitutes for Christ, we are nonetheless expected to follow His example and pray for others.

First Timothy 2:1 says that intercessory prayer should be a part of every Christian's prayer life. The Apostle Paul says, "I exhort therefore, that, first of all, supplications, prayers, intercessions, and giving of thanks, be made for all men." Paul told Timothy that prayers should be offered on behalf of all men, not just some. This is what God expects believers to do.

First Timothy 2:1 says that intercessory prayer should be a part of every Christian's prayer life.

It is common to hear in our prayer groups prayers for everyone from sick children, to missionaries needing to acquire visas, to those who govern our country. We pray for church vision, for the education of our children, for wisdom, and for God's will to be done. We pray for the financing of evangelism projects; we pray for the sending of more missionaries to reach more people; and we pray for opportunities to share the Gospel of Christ with the lost.

We need to understand that praying is expected and important. I have been asked by leaders in other churches whether I thought intercessory prayer was really necessary. My answer is if God expects us to pray, then it is necessary. We do not have to understand why it is necessary. We need only to understand that God wants us to pray for others. And it is always to our personal benefit to obey God.

I am very encouraged when I hear about churches that include prayer groups as part of their ministries. Most of the churches I visit have a time set aside on Sunday or Wednesday for small groups to pray for missionaries. As I visited churches after my recovery from chemotherapy, members I did not even know asked how I was doing. They knew about my battle with cancer and had prayed for me. On bulletin boards in these churches, my prayer letters were posted to keep their members informed about my needs and requests. And every church I visit has a posting of all their missionaries with prayer requests on bulletin boards prominently displayed.

A group of men in our church meet for prayer every Sunday morning before church service, and a time is set for small groups to meet Wednesday evenings for prayer. Throughout the week, some of our church members meet in small groups to pray. For emergency prayer requests, our church members are contacted through email, text messages, and social media. And in our church bulletin, a list of prayer requests is updated each week. What do we pray for? Whatever people ask for and more.

One day when my grandson was eighteen months old and was still learning to walk, he fell backward and hit his head on concrete. He stopped breathing. We called for an ambulance, and we also called the prayer chain. The church was mobilized for emergency prayer on behalf of my grandson. The following Sunday morning, the men's group was still praying for him. I am happy to report that the CT scan showed no injury and that he is an energetic little boy without a care in the world. I thank God for protecting him, and I thank all those who offered their prayers on his behalf.

THE CURSE OF ISRAEL

As I stated before, God expects us to pray for the peace of Israel. And many prayers for Israel's peace have been offered. So some wonder why Israel has been cursed in spite of those prayers. These prayers for peace in Israel are prayers because of revelation. So it is reasonable to expect that these prayers would be granted. But, up to this point, they are not. Yet, prayers because of revelation are guaranteed and backed by the will and power of God. Why then is there no peace in Israel?

There are three things to remember about God's will for Israel. First, Israel *will* be blessed and at peace. That day is coming. It is promised by God and is revealed in His Word. It has not happened yet, but it will. Hebrews 11:39–40 says, "And these all, having obtained a good report through faith, received not the promise: God having provided some better thing for us, that they without us should not be made perfect." Hebrews 11:10 says that Abraham "… looked for a city which hath foundations, whose builder and maker is God."

Second, some of God's promises are fulfilled conditionally. In this case, for Israel to be blessed and be at peace, they needed to believe God and obey Him. Israel's history of being cursed is due to their rebellion against God, their idolatry, and their unbelief. Israel's troubles and lack of peace were predictable and were always preceded by warnings to repent. Nonetheless, there were believing Jews who would be counted as part of the nation of Israel in the future. The Jews, like everyone else, must be changed by the gracious promise of God without the Law. Only with this change will they enter heaven and enjoy an eternity of peace and blessings.

Third, the deliverance of Israel from evil must be according to the will of God. God's will for Israel is that they be blessed. And that will happen, in heaven. But on Earth, Israel was fulfilling a role in God's plan. As a nation under the Old Testament, Israel represented what it meant to have a relationship with God based on Law. Exodus 19:8 is a record of Israel's acceptance of this covenant governing Israel's relationship with God. It says, "And all the people answered together, and said, All that the LORD hath spoken we will do. And Moses returned the words of the people unto the LORD." But a relationship with God based on flawlessly obeying the Law is impossible. Thus, Israel's history after being delivered from Egypt is one curse after another. Israel's role on Earth has been to demonstrate that it is not possible to have a good relationship with God based on Law. Trying to keep the Law is not the way to please God or to qualify to go to heaven. The message of Israel under the Old Testament is how *not* to go to heaven. When Jesus came, He fulfilled the Law. He did what no human could do. And then He replaced the Old Testament with the New Testament (Hebrews 8:6–8). He replaced the Law of human merit with the promise of mercy and grace. The way to have a good relationship with God is to humble yourself to God and rely on His work to qualify you for heaven. You must simply believe that He can and will save you from condemnation.

God delivered Israel from evil to show His grace when they cried out for mercy. And He allowed them to fall prey to evil when they violated the Law and broke their covenant with Him. The blessings and curses of Israel are understandable in light of the covenant they made with God.

On one occasion, Elijah prayed against Israel, but God did not cast them away. The Apostle Paul referenced Elijah's prayer against Israel in Romans 11:2, saying, "God hath not cast away his people which he foreknew. Wot ye not what the scripture saith of Elias? how he maketh intercession to God against Israel...." But God's promise to Israel is that they will reign with Him as a nation forever. This will occur, not now, but later, after the destruction of this world system and only with those who are born-again believers.

DEPENDENCE ON GOD

God requires us to pray in order to be blessed and to change our circumstances. Prayer is not for God. It is for us. He does not need prayer. We need prayer. God has desires, but He has no needs. He desired to create all things and to make us for the purpose of enjoying His blessings. But this was in spite of His eternal contentment. He had no need to create us. He wanted to do it for the pleasure of sharing His blessings.

> *Prayer is not for God. It is for us.*

Our prayers do not persuade God, influence God, or change God in any way. Prayers change us. Prayers remind us and persuade us of what is important. They give us time to reflect on what is truly important about our prayer requests. Prayers help us focus on our priorities. Prayer time is a time of thoughtfulness, and it helps us think about what we really want. It is a time of humility and realization that we are dependent on God.

Praying involves a perspective of reliance on God. We do not tell God what to do. We ask for gracious favors from Him. James 4:2 explains that prayers offered with a lack of humility are not acceptable. "Ye lust, and have not: ye kill, and desire to have,

We do not tell God what to do. We ask for gracious favors from Him.

and cannot obtain: ye fight and war, yet ye have not, because ye ask not." People with arrogant attitudes do not recognize the difference between God's will and their will. They pursue their own ambitions without seeking God's direction. They tell God what to do rather than ask what He wants done. But those who realize their need for God pray unselfishly with humility.

The church at Laodicea is a good example of how Christians can become so self-reliant because of pride that they eventually reject God's help. Revelation 3:20 says, "Behold, I stand at the door, and knock: if any man hear my voice, and open the door, I will come in to him, and will sup with him, and he with me." The church members at Laodicea were proud of their skills and accomplishments. They were wealthy, content, and comfortable. When Christ knocked at the door of their church, they would not open the door to Him because they were doing things their own way. In their minds, they were in control and had no need of God's help. Their previous humility had faded. Now they were proud. They were self-sufficient.

Jesus referred to the last days on Earth as being a time of faithlessness. This means a time is coming when people will fail to understand God and their dependence on Him. They will cease to pray. Jesus asks in Luke 18:8, "Nevertheless when the Son of man cometh, shall he find faith on the earth?" With this question, Jesus indicated that, over time, humanity will see less need for God. As a result, there will be less prayer.

Jesus describes the end days near His coming in Matthew 24:37–38, saying, "But as the days of Noe were, so shall also the coming of the Son of man be. For as in the days that were before the flood they were eating and drinking, marrying and giving in marriage, until the day that Noe entered into the ark." The people of the world will be indulging their lusts and ignoring their spiritual needs. There will be a lack of spiritual discernment. Few will understand the important issues of life in light of the coming judgment day before God. Few will understand their need for God. Fewer will be praying to God. More will be relying on themselves and will be focused on satisfying their lusts.

PRAYER IS FOR US, NOT FOR GOD

God does not need our prayers to know what needs to be done. God does not need our prayers to persuade Him what to do. God cannot be influenced by our prayers. His arm cannot be twisted. He will do that which is according to His will. Prayers do not change God or His mind. Prayers do not change His will. He knows what we need before we ask. He already knows what we want. He already knows His answer. He has known since eternity past our request and His answers. God is not going to change His mind.

If God does not need our prayers, then why does He exhort us to pray? We are exhorted to pray because of the benefits of prayer to us. Prayer gives us an opportunity to participate in making things better. Prayer changes us and the circumstances in our world. Through the exercise of prayer, we build character. We learn to trust Him, and we learn how to discern His will. We are nurtured in our relationship with Him. We receive gifts and blessings from Him. And we help others.

We need to pray because we need God's help. We need to pray because we are dependent on His will and power. We need to pray in order to listen to God and in order to receive wisdom for making decisions, in order to gain insights into life and death and in order to know truth. When we come to a point in which prayer is less important than other things we do, we are failing to recognize the importance of God in our lives to change things. We assume that we can do things ourselves. We assume a self-sufficient, arrogant attitude.

PRAYER CHANGES THINGS

If God does what He wants anyway, some wonder if prayer makes a difference. After all, God will not do anything that is contrary to His will. He only grants prayers that are in accordance to His will. Therefore, it is reasoned that prayers do not change anything.

Does God do anything different because of prayer? Yes. Prayer changes things. This is especially evident with miracles. Miracles are events that are contrary to the natural order of things. Miracles defy the natural laws of creation. This is the reason that miracles are rarely seen. God designed the world perfectly. It is doing what it should be doing. Currently, it is showing the effects of sin in creation. This is important to our learning how bad sin is. Nonetheless, God sometimes intervenes in the natural processes if we make requests. He does so as long as it does not hinder the overall goal to win souls. The winning of the maximum number of souls is the ultimate goal that determines what God will or will not do. Every answer from God can be understood in light of His ultimate goal.

God designed the world perfectly. It is doing what it should be doing. Currently, it is showing the effects of sin in creation.

A young man in our ministry was agonizing over whether God wanted Him to spend Christmas vacation in Fayetteville or in his hometown. He had been praying to seek guidance from the Lord, but he could not determine a definite answer. After talking with him and praying, it became clear to me that God was leaving the choice up to him. Either way, he would be in God's will. This means that neither decision would trigger a chain of events that would diminish the number of souls that could be saved. In this case, God's will allowed for two different paths of life experiences.

The fact that prayers can change our life experiences suggests that there are potentially many paths that we could travel. And because each path is according to God's will, there is more than one path to choose from that would not be sin.

But if we make requests that God grants, we travel down paths of life experiences that deviate from the default path. These alternative paths are prayer paths.

For believers faithfully serving God, multiple paths for our lives suggest that there is a default path of God's will, and there are paths that deviate from this default path due to prayer requests. We follow the default path of God's will when we serve Him obediently without making requests for our own personal desires. It is our choice, according to God's will, to ask or not to ask. But if we make requests that God grants, we travel down paths of life experiences that deviate from the default path. These alternative paths are *prayer paths*. As long as a request does not result in diminishing the number of souls that could be saved now and into the future, those requests granted could lead us down different life paths of experiences. Only God can see the big picture of how different paths for each of our lives will impact the salvation of souls now and into the future. God answers our requests in accordance to fulfilling His desire to save the maximum number of souls.

There are many examples of God answering prayers and changing how things would happen. For example, after Moses pleads for God's mercy on Israel, Numbers 14:20–21 says, "And the LORD said, I have pardoned according to thy word. But as truly as I live, all the earth shall be filled with the glory of the LORD." This verse shows that because of Moses' prayer, God did not judge Israel at that time. The threat of judgment was changed to mercy because of prayer.

The Old Testament records an occasion of rebellion in Israel, when three men, Korah, Dathan, and Abiram, organized a coup against Moses. Numbers 16 records the incident. Moses responded with a challenge to let God show who was right and who was wrong. After everyone gathered together, God told Moses in Numbers 16:21, "Separate yourselves from among this congregation, that I may consume them in a moment." God threatened to judge all the people, but after the people responded by asking for mercy and placed blame on those who incited the rebellion, God changed His threat and spared the congregation. He judged the perpetrators of the rebellion. If they had not prayed for mercy, they would all have been judged. Either way, God's will would have been done. Prayer changed their circumstances.

Amazingly, Numbers 16:41–48 says that the day after God judged Korah and his friends with a miraculous event, the congregation of Israel accused Moses of killing the people of the Lord. God responded to their false accusation by judging them with a plague. As people began dying, Moses responded with prayers of intercession for them. As a result, God stopped the plague of death. He judged Israel for sinning, and then He showed mercy to Israel because of their prayers for forgiveness. God responded to the change of their choices. God *predictably* judged sin as He warned, and He *predictably* showed mercy when atonement was made. He did not change His mind about judgment of sin or about mercy and atonement. The Jews changed their minds; then God changed what He did.

First Kings 21:29 explains why God postponed King Ahab's judgment. Ahab cried to God for mercy, and God said, "Seest thou how Ahab humbleth himself before me? Because he humbleth himself before me, I will not bring the evil in his days...." Because Ahab changed his mind, God changed what He did. Prayer changed things for Ahab.

Suffering is inevitable in a world of sin. But how much suffering could be avoided if more prayers were being made?

Prayer changes things, and without it, a lot more suffering would occur. Suffering is inevitable in a world of sin. But how much suffering could be avoided if more prayers were being made? How many more things could be changed if people were praying? How many more blessings could there be if you and I were praying more frequently? How much better could things have been with more prayer? Those answers will not be known until we get to heaven. And I am afraid the answers will probably shock us. Until then, pray more and pray often! It would be much better to find out in heaven what would have happened if we had not prayed than to find out what did not happen because we did not pray.

CHANGING GOD'S MIND

How many righteous prayers does it take to persuade God to grant our requests? Are a thousand prayers for something more likely to be answered than one prayer? Are a thousand prayers offered by a thousand people more likely to be answered than a thousand prayers offered by one?

The answer to this question involves the point already made about the impossibility of persuading God to do anything. Prayers by people have no power over God. He cannot be bribed. He cannot be bullied. His resistance to our requests cannot be worn down. He cannot have His arm twisted to do that which we ask for. God responds to prayers not out of a need that He has or because of powerful persuasion on our part. God responds to prayers because of the needs we have in the context of His desire to save the maximum number of souls now and in the future.

One prayer or thousands of prayers by one have the same power of persuasion on God: none. Likewise, a million prayers offered by a thousand people have the same power of persuasion on God as one prayer by one person. God's will and power to answer requests remain the same.

If God does not change His mind, then why did Jesus tell the story in Luke 18:1–8 of a widow who persisted in making a request of a judge until the judge granted her request? Why did Jesus encourage the listeners to persist in prayers and not to quit? If God cannot be persuaded and His will cannot be changed, why does Jesus tell us to keep praying until God grants our requests? If the widow had stopped asking, her request would not have been fulfilled. God grants prayers because we have asked. And for some requests, He requires more effort from us. God does not grant prayers because He has been persuaded.

James 4:2 says, "... ye have not, because ye ask not." James 4:3 says, "Ye ask, and receive not, because ye ask amiss." And in some cases, if you are not persistent, you have not (Luke 18:1–8). And sometimes if you do not include fasting, you have not (Matthew 17:21). Because of these conditions, it is proper to think of prayers being granted as a reward for the effort you make rather than as a result of the persuasion you inflict on God. For some requests, God requires more of us before granting our requests.

Being granted prayer requests is about God's persuading us to pray according to His will, rather than our persuading Him to do our will.

So who is persuading whom? Being granted prayer requests is

about God's persuading us to pray according to His will, rather than our persuading Him to do our will.

In our very small and time-limited world of understanding, it is easy to mistakenly think that God changes His mind because He responds to our prayers. But this is our interpretation of how God answers prayers based on how we experience God's answers. God says He answers prayers that are prayed by the righteous who believe in Him without doubt in accordance to His will revealed. Answering our prayers does not mean that we persuaded God to change His mind. It means He answers our prayers in accordance with His will.

Prayers do not change God's will; they change what He will do. If God's will is that sin will be judged, no amount of praying can change His mind. Sin will be judged. If God's will be to show mercy to those who repent, then nothing can prevent Him. If God's will allows for someone to suffer illness unless he prays for healing, then either way in that case, God's will is done. Regardless of what happens because of prayers, God's will is always done.

In my case, I am confident that had I not prayed for healing, I would not have been healed. I prayed first of all for God to reveal to me what His will was. *Should I pray for my life or not?* If I had received the answer no, then I would not have bothered seeing the doctor. I would not have bothered enduring the chemo treatments. But God's answer to me was permission to make my request. He gave me permission to request healing. His will was to take my life if I did not ask for healing, and His will was to heal me if I did ask Him to heal me. Either way, His will would have been done. There were two paths to travel, both of which would have been in His will. I requested the path of healing.

OUR PART IN PRAYING FOR OTHERS

I do not know how many folks were blessed and credited with

sharing in my healing, but there were many. I knew that God answered my prayer to understand the prayers that move mountains and that He was answering my prayer to move my mountain. My mountain was not moved by my power. It was my request to the One who can move mountains. It was also the request of many others. It was God's will and power that made it possible to move my mountain. And God blessed everyone who prayed on my behalf.

People pray when they believe that prayers make a difference and when they care enough about someone else to pray for them. If you struggle with praying for others, you either do not believe prayer will make a difference, or you do not care enough to pray for someone else.

With regard to intercessory prayers, as mentioned before, these are opportunities to share in the credit for helping others. This too is a reward. God makes it possible for unlimited numbers of people to share in unlimited blessings granted to others. More importantly, intercessory prayer is not about personal gain. It is an expression of love for others. It is the fulfillment of God's command to show brotherly kindness and love to others. It is a way to serve others.

Mark 9:14–29 is the account of Jesus' disciples trying to cast a demon out of a boy. Jesus cast the demon out. When the disciples asked Jesus why they could not cast the demon out of the boy, Jesus said, "… This kind can come forth by nothing, but by prayer and fasting." Why does God require more from us for some prayers than for others? After all, the power in prayer is in God. The power of prayer is not in those who offer the prayers or in the number of times a prayer request is made. And whether by one or by many intercessors, God's power to make things happen is always the same. God's infinite power is the same with or without prayers.

The granting of prayers, in some cases, depends on our

dedication and effort. And God requires more of us for some prayers than for others. More is not required of God. More is required of us. Apparently, some requests are more significant or valuable than others. By requiring more of us in our prayers, God is showing us what we are willing to do for some things. We are learning more about ourselves through such experiences. If this be the case, then God is using our prayer experiences to mature us, to persuade us, and to teach us.

But why would God make the granting of some requests depend on the intercessory prayers of others? Why would God put blessings like deliverance from demon possession on hold because others are not offering intercessory prayers correctly? Why would God withhold blessings because others are not praying? To answer this, I remind you of the prayer paths. The default prayer path is still in God's will. We live in a world filled with sin. Everything is happening as it should with the exceptions of interventions by God. So then, if we live without praying for exceptions, we experience what should naturally happen in a world polluted by sin. This is by design. Therefore, changing the natural course of things requires requests from us. If we want change for ourselves or for others, we need to ask God to change what would otherwise be the natural course of events in this world of sin.

In spite of our flaws and feeble abilities to pray, God wants us to pray. He expects us to pray. We are responsible to pray. But the Bible tells us that we do not know how to pray. We are ignorant. We are plagued with a carnal body of flesh, selfishness, and false motivations. These flaws and weaknesses are called infirmities. But God has a remedy. Romans 8:26–27 says, "Likewise the Spirit also helpeth our infirmities: for we know not what we should pray for as we ought: but the Spirit itself maketh intercession for us with groanings which cannot be uttered. And he that searcheth the hearts knoweth what is the mind of the Spirit, because he maketh intercession for the saints according to the will of God." Feeling inadequate or incapable of praying good prayers is not an acceptable excuse to not pray. God wants us to pray. He wants us to pray regardless of our deficiencies. It is the requirement from God that makes one prayer or thousands of prayers by one or by thousands important. He commands us to pray.

God does not require perfect prayers from us or that we pray perfectly. He simply wants us to pray. And as with any commandment, there are rewards, blessings, and benefits that come with obeying God. We won't offer perfect prayers because we can't. We can improve with experience, but God expects us to offer prayers in obedience to Him. In other words, if you feel unqualified, uncertain, and inadequate, but you pray anyway, you are obeying God. God wants our best, but He knows that our best will never be truly good. So the Holy Spirit intercedes on our behalf to edit our prayers to make them right.

As long as God is not telling you to stop asking, you have permission to persist.

If you are persisting in prayer for something God is saying no to, there are two things to keep in mind. First, you do not know how persistent you must be before God says yes. Second, you do not know that God will ever say yes. As long as God is not telling you to stop asking, you have permission to persist. In fact, Jesus admonishes us to keep praying. If you desperately want something, continue praying and never quit.

Ephesians 6:18–20 reminds us ultimately what our prayers should be about: "Praying always with all prayer and supplication in the Spirit, and watching thereunto with all perseverance and supplication for all saints; And for me, that utterance may be given unto me, that I may open my mouth boldly, to make known the mystery of the gospel, For which I am an ambassador in bonds: that therein I may speak boldly, as I ought to speak."

FOR WHAT SHOULD WE PRAY?

Intercessory prayers are offered on behalf of friends, family members, communities, nations, the world, and God's kingdom to come. The Apostle Paul was faithful to offer intercessory prayers for his disciple Timothy. In Second Timothy 1:3, he says, "I thank God, whom I serve from my forefathers with pure conscience, that without ceasing I have remembrance of thee in my prayers night and day." And in Colossians 4:12, he says, "Epaphras, who is one of you, a servant of Christ, saluteth you, always labouring fervently for you in prayers, that ye may stand perfect and complete in all the will of God."

Intercessory prayers can be offered for *any* need and want. For example,

- Intercessory prayers can be offered for healing. Second Samuel 12:16 says that "David therefore besought God for the child; and David fasted, and went in, and lay all night upon the earth."

- Intercessory prayers can be offered for the preservation of spirit, soul, and body. In First Thessalonians 5:23, Paul says, "And the very God of peace sanctify you wholly; and I pray God your whole spirit and soul and body be preserved blameless unto the coming of our Lord Jesus Christ."

- Intercessory prayers can be offered to ask God to forgive unfaithfulness. Second Timothy 4:16 says, "At my first answer no man stood with me, but all men forsook me: I pray God that it may not be laid to their charge."

- Intercessory prayers can be offered to ask God for knowledge and wisdom. Paul writes in Colossians 1:9, "For this cause we also, since the day we heard it, do not cease to pray for you, and to desire that ye might be filled with the knowledge of his will in all wisdom and spiritual understanding."

- Intercessory prayers can be offered to ask God for love to abound in knowledge and discernment. In Philippians 1:9, Paul says, "And this I pray, that your love may abound yet more and more in knowledge and in all judgment."

- Intercessory prayers can be offered to ask God to withhold judgment. God says in Job 42:8, "Therefore take unto you now seven bullocks and seven rams, and go to my servant Job, and offer up for yourselves a burnt offering; and my servant Job shall pray for you: for him will I accept: lest I deal with you after your folly, in that ye have not spoken of me the thing which is right, like my servant Job."

PRAYER THAT FAITH NOT FAIL

In Luke 22:32, Jesus told Peter, "But I have prayed for thee, that thy faith fail not: and when thou art converted, strengthen thy brethren." Jesus' intercessory prayer for Peter was that his *understanding* of who Christ was, of the importance of Christ's death, burial and resurrection, and of the significance of being a witness to others about Christ would not fail.

The word *fail* in this verse means to stop and to cease. If Peter's faith were to fail, he would forget what Jesus had taught and revealed to him. He would forget what was important. He would forget the purpose Christ intended for his life. Therefore, Jesus told Peter that He was praying to His Father in heaven that Peter would be reminded of His words. This would involve the Spirit of God continually revealing to Peter the evidence of things not seen (Hebrews 11:1). Peter would be reminded by faith who Christ was and what His mission was. This was important because of the challenges Peter would be faced with.

At the trial of Jesus Christ, Peter was asked if he was a follower of Jesus. He denied knowing Christ. He was afraid. He was confused by the events and the apparent vulnerability of His

Savior and King. To stand strong in the face of threats to his life, Peter would have to be fully convinced and confident in Christ's message and purpose. He would need to *remember* why he should be unwavering in his commitment to Christ. The prayer of Christ for Peter in Luke 22:32 was important because Peter had to remember Christ's message to make sense out of what was going on.

But Peter also had to be fully persuaded in his own mind that the message of Christ was true. Peter was already converted and saved. He believed and followed Christ. But he still needed to be converted to the *cause* of Christ. Only then could he be unwavering in his commitment to serve Christ and to encourage others to be unwavering as well. This full persuasion is the conversion Christ was referring to. Peter would need to turn from uncertainty and doubt to unwavering commitment. After the resurrection, Peter did convert to unwavering commitment to Christ, and he strengthened others in the faith to do likewise.

We should follow Jesus' example and pray for our faith (revelation of truth) to not fail (fade in memory). We need to pray for others that their faith not fail. This is a prayer God will answer. He wants us to remember and to understand who Christ is and what He expects of us. The question is will we accept this truth and live like it is the only truth?

Such persuasion and deeper conversion to the message of Christ is life changing. Peter's life changed. He dedicated his life to continuing the work of Christ to seek and to save that which was lost. He was fully committed to this task. Peter and the other disciples demonstrated unwavering commitment to God, regardless of the threats. They remained devoted to Christ and His mission even though it cost them their lives. They were devoted to their Savior Jesus Christ with the help of the Holy Spirit, who kept the message of Christ fresh in their thoughts. They not only served Christ for Christ's sake, but they lived for a cause they believed in. They believed in Christ, and they believed in His cause with personal conviction. It became their *own* crusade to share the greatest message in the world with others. With this perspective and commitment, the significance of intercessory prayer is understood and appreciated. Intercessory prayer should include a request that God help everyone keep their faith strong so that they too can understand the most important issues in life.

DELIVERANCE FROM EVIL

In John 17:15, Jesus prayed for His disciples to be delivered from evil. He also instructed His disciples to pray for deliverance from evil (Luke 11:4). This is an important prayer due to the presence of evil and sin in the world. Sin has consequences, just as God warned. The consequences are an inevitable part of our life experiences. For example, even

Failure to pray for deliverance could result in suffering that could have been avoided.

with the intercessory prayers of Jesus, the disciples still suffered the evil of torture and martyrdom. Likewise, Jesus also prayed in the Garden of Gethsemane that the cup of suffering would pass from Him. But He was still crucified. The presence of evil and sin in the world brings inescapable violence and suffering. But prayer reduces the amount of evil and suffering that could occur. Failure to pray for deliverance could result in suffering that could have been avoided. Pray for deliverance from evil, as Jesus and the disciples did.

Evil that God allows to occur is a necessary evil because it is part of the natural consequence of sin. Reducing the consequences of sin in the world is unnatural, but God will grant prayers for deliverance if doing so does not diminish the number of saved souls.

Revelation 6:9–11 says that the prayers of the saints for vengeance against the cruel injustice and persecution of evil in the world will be granted. All prayers for deliverance from evil will be granted. But granting deliverance has been suspended until more souls are saved. Second Peter 3:9 explains, "The Lord is not slack concerning his promise, as some men count slackness; but is longsuffering to us-ward, not willing that any should perish, but that all should come to repentance." It is this goal of saving souls that makes all of God's answers to prayers for deliverance understandable and acceptable. We just need to trust Him. His answers are always the best answers to fulfill His most important goal.

PRAYING SOULS OUT OF HELL

A friend told me that she found it strange how we pray harder to keep people out of heaven than we pray to keep people out of hell. What she meant was that people pray more earnestly for the healing of their Christian friends who are suffering from life-threatening illnesses than for unbelievers who are on the path to eternal condemnation. Praying for the salvation of souls should be no less earnest than praying for the healing of a Christian. The consequences are infinitely different. Life on Earth is temporary. For Christians, it is going to get infinitely and eternally better after this life. For the lost, it is going to be infinitely and eternally worse.

Is it possible to pray for the salvation of souls that are already in hell? No. Hebrews 9:27 says, "And as it is appointed unto men once to die, but after this the judgment." The time to make a choice to believe God is while you are physically alive. Every day and every breath is an extended opportunity to believe and to be saved. Choosing to

Prayers for unbelievers must take place before they die.

delay your decision to believe is choosing risk. God has been warning us of the danger since the foundation of the world. Prayers for unbelievers must take place before they die, and to know what to pray requires understanding God's role, the unbeliever's role, and the intercessor's role in salvation.

Second Peter 3:9 says that God desires that none should perish. First Timothy 2:4 says God wants everyone to be saved. God's role in salvation is to do all the work necessary to save souls. His work begins with "drawing" us. Jesus says in John 6:44, "No man can come to me, except the Father which hath sent me draw him: and I will raise him up at the last day." This "drawing" is God revealing to us His love for us and the need we have for Him. First John 4:19 says that God first loved us. God proved His love by giving His Son as a payment for our sins (John 3:16; Romans 5:8). Romans 10:13–17 shows that God sends messengers to share His invitation for salvation and then confirms this message with faith. These verses show that God initiates and continues to engage in winning the lost, whether we pray or not.

Romans 10:9–17 also shows the role of the lost. To be saved, the lost must believe that Jesus is Lord, that He is risen from the dead, and that He will make believers righteous in order to qualify them to enter heaven (Romans 10:9–11). Believing is the choice God leaves up to every soul.

The role of Christians is to obey God and to share the Gospel message with others. This message is the power of God unto salvation (Romans 1:16). Jesus' message in Mark 1:15 is "...The time is fulfilled, and the kingdom of God is at hand: repent ye, and believe the gospel." Jesus is our example to follow. We should be teaching others about God's message of salvation.

What kinds of prayers were offered for the lost in the Bible? Paul says in Romans 10:1, "Brethren, my heart's desire and prayer to God for Israel is, that they might be saved." This prayer expresses what Paul wants for Israel and shows unity with what God wants and is already doing. It is a generalized prayer asking God to do whatever it takes to save the people of Israel. In Romans 9:3, Paul says that he was even willing to sacrifice his own life if that would save Israel. Paul understood that the experiences of evil and death could possibly lead to the salvation of souls. He was willing to pay the price.

In Matthew 9:38, Jesus says to "Pray ye therefore the Lord of the harvest, that he will send forth labourers into his harvest." We know that God has already sent and is sending witnesses into the world. So Jesus is telling us that we should pray for what God wants and is already doing. God is giving us opportunity to join Him in the calling and sending of witnesses to win souls. Churches can also pray for laborers in order to increase their membership. But the called laborers must also choose to obey God. And part of each laborer's responsibility is to pray for more laborers.

Because Christians are called to be ambassadors for Christ in the world, we should pray for opportunities to share the Gospel and for the ability to clearly teach the Gospel. First Corinthians 3:6 says that we as Christians should sow and water (share and teach) the message of the Gospel of Jesus Christ. God gives the increase. The bottom line is we should pray to be expert witnesses for Christ.

MANAGING MANY REQUESTS

If there are a thousand prayer requests, how do you find time to pray for every single one? There are 1,440 minutes in a day. If you spent a minute for each request, you could offer 720 requests in half a day. Jesus did not spend half a day in prayer most of the time, although Luke 6:12 does mention an occasion when He spent all night in prayer. And by studying the content of His prayers, we can see that He spent time in prayer glorifying His Father. In the model prayer He gave to His disciples in Matthew 6:9–13, the first four points are directed to God and are about His kingdom. The next three points are about personal needs. Then the end of the prayer is about God and His kingdom again. Following is the list of prayer points Jesus included in His instructions.

1. Our Father which art in heaven,
2. Hallowed be thy name.
3. Thy kingdom come.
4. Thy will be done in earth, as it is in heaven.
5. Give us this day our daily bread.
6. And forgive us our debts, as we forgive our debtors.
7. And lead us not into temptation, but deliver us from evil:
8. For thine is the kingdom, and the power, and the glory, forever.

The mentioning of us shows that intercessory prayers as well as personal requests should be offered. Christ is still interceding for us. Romans 8:34 says, "Who is he that condemneth? It is Christ that died, yea rather, that is risen again, who is even at the right hand of God, who also maketh intercession for us." Obviously, Jesus was not giving the disciples an exhaustive list of things to pray for. But the things He does mention are all the more important to take note of because they are mentioned.

How can prayers be offered when the things to pray for are more numerous than the minutes in a day? A review of prayers in the Bible shows that prayers are both detailed and generalized. For example, in John 11:42, Jesus prays to His Father about the raising of Lazarus. In Mark 9:29, Jesus says that difficult things require specific prayer and effort. But in John 17:9, Jesus prays in general for the disciples as a group. The great prayer prophet Daniel prayed in general for the nation of Israel (Daniel 9:20). And in First Timothy 2:1, Paul says, "I exhort therefore, that, first of all, supplications, prayers, intercessions, and giving of thanks, be made for all men." This helps us think about praying for many requests.

There is no formula for how many prayers to pray every day. God wants us to pray specific and generalized prayers. There is no formula for how many prayers to pray every day. Throughout the Scriptures, some prayed in the morning, in the afternoon, and in the evening. There is no command when and how often. This means that it is up to you to listen to God telling you how often He wants you to pray and how specific your prayers should be.

A prayer network is a great way to manage prayer requests and coordinate intercessors. Prayer chains are a very good way to send out emergency prayer requests. Keeping a personal prayer list is helpful. Some churches use their bulletin to list prayer requests along with ministry activities. Rotating through a prayer list over a week or even a month is useful for large prayer lists. God does not tell us how to manage prayer requests or how to incorporate prayers and intercessions into our lives. What He requires of us is that we pray.

PRAYER AND SUPPORT FOR ME

When I was battling cancer and undergoing chemotherapy treatments, the intercessory prayer chains and networks went around the world. Friends in churches and on the mission fields let me know they were praying for me. It was encouraging to hear from them. Most importantly, it was encouraging to know that God was hearing from them too.

Along with the prayers of intercession, we received cards,

letters, gifts, food, and flowers from around the world. Students from the school wrote me notes. Friends called. Some people I did not know wrote me just to let me know that they were praying for me. I even had Buddhists and some folks who were not sure there was a God praying for me. Some non-religious friends were "pulling for me." I was amazed at the outpouring of love, kindness, and care that was shown.

For me, brief weekly calls were appreciated. But I had a couple of friends who just let me talk and tell them how I was really doing. That was a great ministry to me, and I told them so. I thanked them for being there to listen. It was therapy for me just to share some of the pains I was experiencing and how I was feeling.

My encouragement folder became packed quickly. I did not save all the notes, and now I wish I had. They were important to me, but now that my trial is a distant memory, they are more important to me.

I received a lot of advice and suggestions, which I truly appreciated. Though some of the advice was misguided, I truly appreciated the fact that people cared enough to try to be a help to me. I received books, magazines, and online articles. I received bottles of pills and packages of herbs. Some of them I tried, and others I did not. But for each gift of love, I said thank you with sincere gratitude.

People offered their help, and some seemed willing to do anything for me. A good friend brought me malted shakes each week as an encouragement. Malts were one of my favorite drinks, and he knew that. But after several weeks, I had to tell him I did not want any more. The problem with chemotherapy is that some things become associated with not feeling good. I had read that some people stopped eating certain foods because they became associated with the nausea. Even the sight or smell of some things triggers nausea.

I asked the nurse one time if anyone ever got sick just from looking at her. She laughed and said no. But she said that a few people got sick when they drove up to the office and looked at the building. My triggers were limited to just a few foods like malt, macaroni and cheese, and jello. It took a year or so to regain a taste for these things.

Rubbing alcohol and betadine were the worst triggers of my nausea, and unfortunately, I could not escape them. These were used to clean the port-a-cath area of skin before treating me, and the smell sickened me. Even now, the thought of smelling these things turns my stomach. I can tolerate them, but I prefer not to smell them. This is one of the reasons having mint gum or candy was helpful. They masked the smell of the antiseptics. I didn't eat the mints. I just took the cap off and sniffed them. It helped a lot.

Naturally, my family and church members were very helpful. My parents and Colleen's mother took turns coming to Arkansas from California to help us. They were a big help, especially at the beginning when we did not know what to expect. They mostly helped take care of the baby. Friends helped me with routine maintenance around the house. A young man in the church kept my lawn mowed in the summer. My brother and his boys came from Texas to rake leaves in November. Friends from church took me to a Chinese restaurant for my birthday.

My sister in California sent me a book titled *Where the Buffaloes Roam: Building a Team for Life's Challenges* by Bob Stone. It had good ideas in it about setting up a support team, and my sister organized one for me. Many of my sister's friends wrote letters of encouragement and sent tips for how to cope with treatment. I appreciated it all very much.

A man who battled with cancer ten years earlier told me that people mean well and start out with support but then leave you. They ask how you are doing but are not really interested. In other words, his experience was one of feeling abandoned. I have heard of that for others, but my experience was one of great support—consistent and genuine.

Being in a church that is more like a family than a religious institution, I was surrounded by a powerful support group. Family, friends, and church were with me. I appreciate each one very much.

But during those times when I was in my room by myself, I never felt alone. God was always with me, and I knew folks were thinking about me and praying for me. I could call for help at any time if needed, and someone would respond. In fact, when I needed a blood transfusion, twenty-two men volunteered to donate blood. That is the kind of support I had. I had great friends, a great church, a wonderful family to intercede for me, and a marvelous God who comforted me.

GREAT INSIGHTS TO REMEMBER

1. Prayers offered on behalf of someone else are called intercessory prayers.

2. People pray when they believe that prayers work and when they care enough about someone else to pray for them.

3. Intercessory prayers are a way of multiplying blessings to many people.

4. Prayer is not for God. It is for us. God does not need prayer. We need prayer.

5. Prayers do not change God or His will. Prayers change us.

6. God has known since eternity past your requests and His answers.

7. Prayers change the natural course of events in God's design of creation.

8. Prayer gives us an opportunity to participate in making things better.

9. We need prayers because we need God.

10. Every answer from God can be understood in light of His ultimate goal to save the maximum number of souls.

11. Prayers do not change God's will; they change what He will do.

12. Prayer makes alternative life paths possible without diminishing the number of souls to be saved.

13. Prayer changes things, and without it, a lot more suffering would occur.

14. One prayer or thousands of prayers by one have the same power of persuasion on God.

15. Prayers are granted not because we influenced God to change His mind but because we put effort into the prayers.

16. Intercessory prayer is an expression of love for others.

17. Changing the natural consequence of things requires requests from us.

18. Persistent prayer is for our benefit, not for increasing influence over God.

19. Persistent prayer benefits us with reflection on what we really want.

20. Prayer benefits us in five ways.

    a. First, prayer reminds us of our dependence on God. We need God. We must rely on Him.

    b. Second, being granted a request desired brings pleasure. We will not receive some things if we do not ask. God requires us to ask. James 4:2 says, "... yet ye have not, because ye ask not." There are benefits to be enjoyed if we pray, and they are sometimes missed because we did not pray.

c. Third, praying nurtures our relationship with God because of the time spent with Him. Relationships form and are nurtured with time spent together. This is the same with God as it is with people. My time in prayer strengthens my relationship with God and my commitment to Him.

d. Fourth, our requests made to God help us to stay focused on what is really important. Time spent in prayer is time addressing needs and asking for wisdom and guidance. It is time devoted to acknowledging God and honoring Him.

e. Fifth, prayer is a way for God to share with us the blessing of helping others. Through prayer, God makes it possible for us to share in the innumerable blessings occurring every day in others' lives. First Samuel 30:24 says, "For who will hearken unto you in this matter? but as his part is that goeth down to the battle, so shall his part be that tarrieth by the stuff: they shall part alike."

5
PRAYERS BECAUSE GOD ANSWERED

And all things, whatsoever ye shall ask in prayer,
believing, ye shall receive.
—Matthew 21:22

One of the most desired experiences in the Christian life is to be granted your prayer requests. Prayers granted affirm your relationship with God. You are encouraged by the realness of interacting with God. You feel confident about your spirituality. And the reward of God's manifested pleasure feels good.

Imagine being able to expect God's approval for every prayer request. That would be exciting. That would give you something to look forward to in your prayer goals every day.

Is it even possible to expect every prayer to be granted? Psalm 37:4–5 says, "Delight thyself also in the LORD; and he shall give thee the desires of thine heart. Commit thy way unto the LORD; trust also in him; and he shall bring it to pass."

I wanted the experience of receiving whatever I desired. I was focused on prayers that move mountains, but the idea of praying and receiving whatever I asked for intrigued me. I puzzled over how my personal experience did not match up with the promises made in the Bible in this regard. I asked for many things that were not granted.

But God did grant my prayer to understand more about praying. And what I discovered was that God *was* answering all of my prayers. The problem was that I was not recognizing the answers. I am excited to share with you how you can recognize God's answers. I will also show you the difference between receiving the desires of your heart and receiving whatever you pray for.

Do you know the experience of God giving you whatever you ask for? If not, why not? What do you expect from God when you pray? What would you like to expect from God when you pray?

If you are like everyone else, you want to know that your prayers are being heard. You want to know that your prayers are not a waste of time. You want to know that your prayers will get answered. You want to move mountains. You want more than this. You want to know that, whatever your requests are, they will be *granted*.

Would predictable and consistently answered prayers motivate you to pray more? I have heard people respond with an enthusiastic yes to that question. It is important to ask these questions and admit disappointment rather than deny that we are disappointed with our prayers. Why? Because when you are in denial, there is nothing to fix. Until you are ready to admit there is a problem, you will not seek a solution.

GOD'S PROMISE TO GRANT WHAT YOU WANT

If you believe in Jesus Christ as your Lord and Savior, you believe in prayer. And if you believe in prayer, then you believe that God hears your prayers. The question is will He *grant* your prayers?

Getting to the point of having all of my prayers granted is what I was searching for when I asked God to teach me about the prayers that move mountains. My experience was that sometimes prayers were answered, and at other times, it appeared that they were not answered. It appeared to me that prayers were arbitrarily answered. There was no explanation for why some prayers were answered and others were not. In my mind, it seemed reasonable to expect consistency in receiving answers.

When my prayers were not answered, it made me wonder why. First John 5:15 says, "And if we know that he hear us, whatsoever we ask, we know that we have the petitions that we desired of him." I knew God heard my prayers. How could He not? He is God. He knows everything. Further, many of my prayers had been answered. So I had no reason to think that God was not hearing my prayers. If He were answering some of my prayers, then I had reason to expect Him to answer all of my prayers. If God were hearing my prayers, according to First John 5:15, all of my prayers should be answered. The promise in that verse is not that *some* or *most* petitions would be granted. I expected *all* of my petitions to be answered, as the Bible promised.

In Matthew 21:22, Jesus said, "And all things, whatsoever ye shall ask in prayer, believing, ye shall receive." I was asking, and I believed. I put the promise of this verse and others to the test by asking and getting rid of all doubt in my mind. I heard others call this "name and claim," so that is what I did. But like many who do this, my prayers were not granted. What was the problem?

THE PROBLEM WITH US

Verses that promise that we will receive whatever we ask for are not real in our lives. What is the problem? The problem is not with the promises. The problem is with us.

I discovered that the problem with those who experience what they call "unanswered" prayers is ignorance. I know that sin is a reason for "unanswered" prayers, but I am not talking to those struggling with sin. I am talking to those who want to live for God and are seeking to make their prayer lives a success. They desire to live for God and want the experience of having their prayers granted. I was fully committed to serving God and living for Him. I was seeking ways to make my life better in serving Him, and I was seeking ways to make my prayer life better.

Is it possible to love God and still be ignorant? Yes. Loving God does not mean we are mature. A child loves his mother yet lacks maturity and knowledge. With time to grow, we will learn how to recognize God's answers.

After studying all the verses I could find that promise we can be granted whatever we ask for, I discovered that every verse with such a promise includes a condition. For example, Matthew 21:21–22 and Mark 11:22–23 say to have faith in God. John 14:13 and John 15:16 include the requirement to pray in the name of Christ. First John 3:22 says to keep His commandments. All of the conditions for receiving whatever we ask for can be summed up as *praying in God's will.*

The conditions for receiving our prayer requests are very clear. But the conditions are not easily understood or recognized until we study the promises carefully. It is easy to spot the promise (to receive whatever we want) and to focus on this one part of a verse to the neglect of the conditions for receiving whatever we ask for.

God is not the one to blame for our frustration and

disappointment with prayer. James 4:3 says, "Ye ask, and receive not, because ye ask amiss, that ye may consume it upon your lusts." Praying amiss is explained as making requests of God to fulfill our lusts. In other words, selfish prayers are not granted.

Prayers for satisfying the lust of the eyes, the lust of the flesh, and the pride of life can appear different to different people. There are people who pray selfishly for their enrichment and stature. They are greedy and covetous. Others are vengeful and pray for the harm of others.

Some are religious, such as the Pharisees in Jesus' day, who pray selfishly for their religious achievements and for attention from others. Again, the problem is that these prayers are not according to God's will.

Some religious people pray like they are praying to a tree or a rock or a mountain. In their quest to get what they want from God, they resort to ritualizing their prayers or to creating self-inflicted hardship to convince God of their willingness to suffer in return for a favorable answer from Him. These are prayer formulas invented by ignorant men seeking to get God's attention and to convince Him to grant their requests. There is no life in their ritualized prayers. These prayers might be intended for God, but they are not directed to God. They are prayers of method, not of a relationship with God.

Speaking of lifelessness, there are religious people who pray to false gods, who are not gods. These prayers are lifeless because they are prayers to lifeless entities. There is no conversation. Lifeless, fictional gods do not communicate. And when prayers are directed to a different god, the true God of heaven is not going to answer on their behalf. We should not be surprised that God does not answer prayers that are not directed to Him.

Ignorance of *how* God answers is another problem that contributes to our frustration. If we do not understand what to look for, then we fail to see the answer. In order to recognize God's answers, we need to know what God's answers look like. We need to study God's Word and learn God's way to overcome ignorance.

Another reason for not recognizing God's answers is the problem of not wanting to accept God's answers. We do not listen to Him because we expect Him to answer us as we have requested. When we look for the answer we want, it is easy to miss the answer God gives.

Prayers that do not work are discouraging. We cannot help but wonder what is wrong and be disappointed. If our prayers are frustrating due to sin, then let the error of our ways be known. Pray to know the problem and the solution. God wants to answer these prayers. He wants us to know how to pray. He wants us to experience answers to every prayer.

Why pray the same way expecting different results? Pray differently. Learn how to change. Study the Bible, and pray for instruction. Stop praying the same way that fails. Don't quit praying. Just change the way you pray.

You are probably thinking at this point, "This is the reason I am reading this book." You are trying to learn. You are willing to change the way you pray. You are just wondering what changes to make. Learning is required to successfully change. Through study and prayer, you are already changing. As I said, God wants your prayers to be successful. This is good news. He will answer your prayer to know how to pray. He answered my prayer to know, and He is still teaching me.

I discovered that learning more about prayer adjusted my expectations. I discovered what the answers to the four types of prayer look like, and this helped me recognize the answers to every prayer. And I discovered that, when I adjusted my expectations to the way God answers different kinds of prayer, I was no longer disappointed and frustrated.

Change but do not quit learning about prayer. You never know how close you are to a new insight. You don't want to be like the man who swam halfway across the English Channel and turned back because he did not know if he could make it the rest of the way. Always push forward in learning and praying to know more about prayer.

If you are expecting to reach the point of having every prayer for a personal desire granted, then I applaud you. I have not arrived at that point yet. However, I have learned that God answers every prayer. That insight was a big boost of encouragement for me. Even recognizing the answer *no* is more encouraging than thinking that God is ignoring me. Are you expecting miracles every time you pray? Then consider this. The fact that the God of creation even responds to you is a miracle. And granted prayers are miracles that change what would have normally happened.

RECEIVING THE DESIRES OF YOUR HEART

When God has your heart, your prayers are granted. Loving God means that you love His ways. His will is your will. His goals are your goals. His concerns are your concerns. This unity with God brings unity in desires and prayers. When God has your heart, you pray the prayers that Jesus would pray.

My heart's desire was to understand the prayers that move mountains and to receive whatever I requested. I knew by faith and from the Word of God that God wanted me to understand how to pray successfully. God wants everyone to understand and experience prayers that move mountains and prayers that are always answered. Why? Because the promises in the Bible are for everyone. That means everyone missing the experience of such prayers should ask God for instruction.

There is no better example to look to for insights into prayers being granted than Jesus. In John 11:22, Martha said to Jesus, "But I know, that even now, whatsoever thou wilt ask of God, God will give it thee." How would you like to be able to pray like Jesus and have whatever you pray for granted? It is possible, if you pray like Jesus.

Jesus received whatever He prayed for because He prayed for what His Father wanted. Jesus and His Father were one. They were in perfect unity to the point of being indistinguishable. Jesus told Philip in John 14:9, "… He that hath seen me hath seen the Father…." When Jesus prayed, He was praying as His Father would.

If you want your prayers granted, you must pray like Jesus would. This requires knowing Him very well. He must be your best friend. You must learn to think like Him and share His desires and perspectives. His goals must be your goals. When you are in unity with Christ in this way, then you will want what He wants, and you will pray for the things He would pray for.

When you want what God wants, then *every prayer* will be granted. But this does not mean that *every request* will be granted.

Every prayer includes at least two requests. For example, you could *pray* for rain to end a drought in California. The obvious *request* is for rain. The other *request* is for your desire that God's will be done. If God does not want rain, that *request* will not be granted, but your *prayer* will be granted because you want what God wants. When you discover that God's will is to not allow rain, His answer becomes your desire too. Even though your initial request for rain is denied, your prayers for God's will to be done are always granted. God answers every prayer according to His will. In other words, every answer from God is always His will. If you desire God's will to be done, then every prayer is granted, even if the specific request be denied.

Wanting what God wants does not mean that you know every

detail of His will. This means that it is possible to want what God wants but not know what He wants until you ask. You want whatever His answer is. Therefore, requests made by those who desire God's will to be done are always offered with the additional request, spoken or unspoken, that His will be done.

In anticipation of His death, Jesus prayed in John 12:27, "Now is my soul troubled; and what shall I say? Father, save me from this hour: but for this cause came I unto this hour." In the Garden of Gethsemane, Jesus prayed to His Father, saying in Luke 22:42, "… if thou be willing, remove this cup from me: nevertheless not my will, but thine, be done." Jesus was making His request in anticipation of His dreadful suffering. His agony is mentioned in Luke 22:43–44, "And there appeared an angel unto him from heaven, strengthening him. And being in an agony he prayed more earnestly: and his sweat was as it were great drops of blood falling down to the ground."

Jesus agonized over the thought of the suffering He was about to endure. He prayed earnestly for deliverance and strength as the time for His death drew closer. "His sweat was as it were great drops of blood falling down to the ground." This describes the flow of sweat being like blood flowing from a wound. He was not just perspiring. Sweat was not just dripping. It was flowing. The agony Jesus was experiencing at this time is indescribable. The excruciating, infinite pain He was about to suffer is beyond description. But here was Jesus, the Christ, God's Son, God manifested in the flesh, in indescribable agony.

Jesus prayed, "Father… if thou be willing, remove this cup from me: nevertheless not my will, but thine, be done." There are two mutually exclusive requests being made: 1) "Remove this cup" was His request to be delivered from the experience of death, and 2) "Not my will, but thine." Jesus was dreading the excruciating pain and the horrible death of eternal condemnation. He dreaded it. But He came to Earth as a man to do just that. He came to suffer eternal condemnation. He did not want to suffer, but there was no other way to save mankind from sin. The wages of sin is eternal death. To pay this debt ourselves would take forever. There would be no salvation. But being God, Jesus could pay an infinite debt instantly. He wanted to save our souls, so He volunteered to pay our debt. He did not want to suffer, but He wanted to save us. To fulfill one desire meant not fulfilling the other. These are mutually exclusive desires.

To resolve mutually exclusive desires, the greater desire must be chosen. In this case, Jesus chose to suffer damnation on our behalf. His greatest desire was to do His Father's will, which was to save our souls. Though He asked His Father to deliver Him from the experience, He also asked that His Father's will be done, saying, "Nevertheless not my will, but thine, be done." Obviously, this was also Jesus' will according to John 12:27. And in John 4:34, Jesus said, "My meat is to do the will of him that sent me, and to finish his work."

This conflict between mutually exclusive desires in Jesus is shared with us in the Bible to show the agony Christ was facing. He did not want to suffer, but He was willing to because there was no other way to help us. This conflict in Jesus shows that He loved us more than He dreaded eternal damnation. His infinite love for us is greater than the suffering of eternal death. By choosing the greater desire, which was to make salvation possible for us, His desire was fulfilled. The desire of His heart was granted. He received what He prayed for.

When we love God and delight in Him, our greatest desire is that God's will be done. Regardless of the requests made to God, those who love God pray "Not my will, but Thy will be done." When you pray this way, God's response is to grant every prayer.

This insight into prayer answers helps us understand why the promise in Psalm 37:4–5 is always true. "Delight thyself also in the LORD; and he shall give thee the desires of thine heart. Commit thy way unto the LORD; trust also in him; and he shall bring it to pass."

Another example of mutually exclusive requests is Paul's request for the removal of a "thorn in his flesh" (Second Corinthians 12:7). A thorn in the flesh is an expression that means there was an annoyance in his life that was distracting him. He identifies this thorn as a messenger from Satan who was harassing him. But because Paul delighted in the Lord, he also wanted God's will to be done in his life. Paul desired two mutually exclusive things. God denied Paul's request, and yet Paul says he gloried in the answer. Why? Because God's will was done. That was Paul's greater desire. When we desire God's will to be done, every prayer is granted and acceptable.

Only in delighting in the Lord and wanting His will to be done can you receive *every* desire of your heart. When you delight in the Lord, every answer from God is the desire of your heart, and the timing of every answer is acceptable. Though every request may not be granted, the desire for God's will is always granted. Those who delight in the Lord want nothing less than God's will to be done.

You do not have to be sinful to be told no. You can be in God's will and desire that God's will be done and be told no. Jesus was not sinning when He asked His Father to deliver Him. Paul was not sinning when he asked God to remove the thorn from his flesh. Both desired that God's will be done. Both desired to fulfill God's plan. Their purpose in life was God's purpose.

God gives us permission to ask whatever we want. There is nothing wrong with asking God for something you think would be good for your ministry and for fulfilling God's purpose in your life. Delighting in the Lord does not mean that you automatically understand the details of what God wants you to pray for. Desiring God's will does not require the omniscience of God to know what you can and cannot ask for. Being of finite mind, you must ask to find out what God will grant, so you should not be surprised if He says no.

THE REWARDS OF KNOWING AND DOING GOD'S WILL

Desiring God's will guarantees that every prayer will be granted. Do you want God's will to be done in your life?

When we pray to know God's will for our lives, He rewards us by revealing His will. Knowing God's will is a reward for asking. If we do not ask, then we are not blessed with knowing His will. God requires that we ask. Rewards are not compensations like wages. Wages are what you earn. Rewards are bonuses. They are given to encourage. They are not given because you deserve them.

For those who desire to know God's will in order to do His will, it is rewarding to have His will revealed. There is pleasure in knowing what God wants us to do because there is pleasure in doing His will. And with the pleasure of knowing, we are also rewarded with confidence and boldness that comes with knowing we are doing what He desires.

What is a reward? Is it a ribbon? A trophy? A plaque? A pin for your lapel? Is it recognition? Is it appreciation for what you have done? These things can be rewards. But unlike an award, a *reward* is more intrinsic. A reward is something that blesses you, whether or not anyone commends you. Though you may not receive an award, you still can be rewarded due to the pleasure and satisfaction you receive.

God rewards us for what we do. He does not reward us for doing something better than anyone else. There will not be an award ceremony in heaven to hand out crowns and trophies for the best witness, the most generous, the most miracles. Rather there will be rewards for what you do because you did right.

Rewards are blessings that we receive for doing something. Rewards are blessings because God designed us to enjoy rewards. We receive pleasure from being rewarded, and this incentivizes us to do more things that reward us. God's approval when we do well is a reward because it produces pleasure in us.

In First Corinthians 3:8, Paul spoke of rewards based on what Christians do, saying, "Now he that planteth and he that watereth are one: and every man shall receive his own reward according to his own labour." God rewards His servants according to what they do. This has nothing to do with their salvation because salvation is the work of God. But what they do after being saved is rewarded.

Paul explains in First Corinthians 9:17 another way to be rewarded, "For if I do this thing willingly, I have a reward: but if against my will, a dispensation of the gospel is committed unto me." In other words, if we serve God willingly, we are rewarded with the blessing of knowing that we have done what is good and right. He contrasts the willingness to preach the Gospel with just doing it begrudgingly because it has to be done. If we serve unwillingly, there is no satisfaction or pleasure, just duty. The lesson to learn is that, if you are going to serve God, do it cheerfully and wholeheartedly. He will reward you by revealing His pleasure and approval.

In Matthew 6:5–6, Jesus describes how *attention* is a reward, saying, "And when thou prayest, thou shalt not be as the hypocrites are: for they love to pray standing in the synagogues and in the corners of the streets, that they may be seen of men. Verily I say unto you, They have their reward. But thou, when thou prayest, enter into thy closet, and when thou hast shut thy door, pray to thy Father which is in secret; and thy Father which seeth in secret shall reward thee openly." Those who pray to impress others get their reward of attention. Those who pray to God get their reward from Him. Successful prayer is to gain God's attention and approval.

Jesus refers to another reward in Matthew 10:41, saying, "He that receiveth a prophet in the name of a prophet shall receive a prophet's reward; and he that receiveth a righteous man in the name of a righteous man shall receive a righteous man's reward." God rewards those who befriend and who host those who serve God. He does not describe the details of the reward, but there is a reward.

Seek to know what God is willing to reward you with. If you don't ask, you will not receive the reward of knowing. Ask for everything and anything that is good and in agreement with His will. If it is God's will, He will grant it. If you do not ask, you will never know what could have been.

For Christians, there is no compensation. God owes us nothing. He has already given His life for us to make the hope of eternal life possible. It was all grace and only by grace. We did not deserve salvation, and we deserve nothing more after being saved. But God loves us. His desire to bless us goes beyond the grace of salvation. He has more that He wants to give us. These blessings are rewards, not because we deserve rewards, but because He wants to shower us with blessings.

As servants of God, we have the responsibility to serve Him. First Corinthians 4:2 says, "Moreover it is required in stewards, that a man be found faithful." We should live for Him. It is the right thing to do. It is good for us. We repented because we wanted Him to be our Lord. There is nothing to be compensated for. Luke 17:9–10 emphasizes this fact, saying, "Doth he thank that servant because he did the things that were commanded him? I trow not. So likewise ye, when ye shall have done all those things which are commanded you, say, We are unprofitable servants: we have done that which was our duty to do."

If any blessings come with serving Christ, thank God for His love and grace. He makes more blessings possible only because of

His love for us, not because we deserve them. There is nothing we can do to make God owe us anything. We will always be eternally indebted to Him.

GOD ANSWERS EVERY PRAYER IMMEDIATELY

Is it really possible to pray and experience an answer to every prayer? Yes. Does this require doing something special? No. God answers every prayer He hears. He answers the prayers of the lost and of the saved.

God answers every prayer immediately with the appropriate answer according to His will. In fact, sometimes God answers prayers before requests are made. In John 16:19, the disciples were wondering what Jesus meant when He said He was leaving them but would return. "Now Jesus knew that they were desirous to ask him, and said unto them, Do ye enquire among yourselves of that I said, A little while, and ye shall not see me: and again, a little while, and ye shall see me?" God indeed hears and answers every prayer.

In First Samuel 1:27, a childless woman named Hannah was granted her prayer request. She said, "For this child I prayed; and the LORD hath given me my petition which I asked of him." Her child was a granted prayer request. God finally said yes. This is the answer we all want to hear from God. Hannah was so excited about God saying yes that she thanked the Lord and dedicated her son to serving God, which he gladly did. But was God's answer immediate?

According to the story, Hannah had prayed for a child for at least four years, if not more (First Samuel 1:4–7). Annually, Hannah prayed for a child, but she remained childless. This was God's immediate answer. She prayed the *prayer of personal desire*, and God said *no, not yet.* Eventually, she had a child. God was not ignoring Hannah. He was not failing to answer her prayers during the years of her being childless. He was telling her no, not yet.

After Jesus was told that his friends Mary and Martha were asking Him to heal their sick brother, Lazarus, Jesus was silent and stayed away until Lazarus died. In John 11:15, Jesus explained, "… I am glad for your sakes that I was not there, to the intent ye may believe…." Mary and Martha wanted Jesus to keep their brother alive, but Jesus was planning to raise Lazarus from the dead. He had a different plan for Lazarus. Therefore, His silent answer to Mary and Martha was *no*, He would not heal him. He would not grant their request. Jesus answered their prayers immediately with His silence.

Why did Jesus leave Mary and Martha in suspense? He did not do this all the time, but on this occasion He did. His immediate answer of *no* increased the sense of hopelessness for Lazarus. People presumed that Lazarus was beyond help once he died. There was no hope of recovering him from death. It was too late. John 11:21 says, "Then said Martha unto Jesus, Lord, if thou hadst been here, my brother had not died." When Jesus told Martha that Lazarus would rise again, she acknowledged that she believed he would be raised in the last days. But Martha, Mary, and others had given up hope for Lazarus being alive again in the flesh.

Jesus' silent answer made the raising of Lazarus even more amazing due to the hopelessness that everyone felt. If Jesus had sent word saying *yes* or even *no, not yet*, the hopelessness would have been lessened. Therefore, Jesus did not reveal His intentions prior to raising Lazarus. He allowed His silent answer to be thought of as a definite no. Jesus wanted to make it clear that nothing was impossible for Him. In Him, there is always hope. Hope is eternal. What a tremendous lesson!

The example of Martha and Mary shows that trusting God is imperative. He hears our prayers, and He answers our prayers. His answers may not be what we are looking for, and so we do not recognize His answers. We may interpret His silence as a non-answer. But this is not the case. We need to trust God that He is in control, that He answers every prayer, that every answer is the best answer, and that all things work together for good to them that love God. When we accept these truths about God, we will recognize His answers immediately and accept them.

God answers every prayer immediately. Even silence is an answer. When Mary and Martha sent messengers to Jesus to ask Him to heal their brother, He already knew His answer was no. His response of silence to them was His answer.

WHEN IT SEEMS GOD DOES NOT ANSWER

As stated above, there is no such thing as an unanswered prayer. God answers every prayer, and every answer is immediate.

What we call unanswered prayers are really answered prayers. Sometimes they are *silent answers*, and other times they are *unrecognized answers*. The issue is not about whether God answers our requests, but whether we recognize the answers.

An "unanswered" prayer would mean that possibly God requires *time to think* about our requests. I put *unanswered* in quotation marks to indicate that this is how it is perceived by some, not how it really is. God does not require time to think about prayer requests. He does not need time to ponder the best answer. He already knows the answer He will give before we ask. He already knows our needs, wants, and prayers before we do. Jesus said in Matthew 6:8, "… for your Father knoweth what things ye have need of, before ye ask him." He knew our questions and His answers before He created the world. He does not have to wait for our requests, and He does not have to spend more time thinking about His answers. If God's answer has already been determined before you ask, you cannot get an answer more immediate than this.

An "unanswered" prayer would also mean that possibly God is not *listening* to us pray. But since God is omniscient, then He must know everything, including every prayer request. The fact is that God hears every prayer of both the lost and the saved. He hears all the prayers offered to false gods. He knows every sin and every sinful thought. He knows every thought, whether prayed or not. He knows everything. He is God. The fact is that God hears every prayer and immediately answers every prayer that is directed to Him. Obviously, He does not bother answering prayers directed to false gods. He lets them answer for themselves.

God not only knows the answer to every prayer before we pray, He knows *how* He will answer every request. Nothing can prevent His answers. Even a delayed answer is a deliberate answer.

If God answers every prayer, what about verses that say God will not hear? For example, Job 35:13 says, "Surely God will not hear vanity, neither will the Almighty regard it." And Psalm 66:18 says, "If I regard iniquity in my heart, the Lord will not hear me." These verses use anthropomorphism, a human attribute, to describe God's response to prayers He disapproves of. For example, in an argument, one person might respond by saying, "I do not hear a thing you are saying." Obviously, he does hear what is being said. What he means is "I do not care what you are saying" and "What you have to say is not important to me." Because God actually hears every prayer, these verses are saying that God will not honor the prayers of the arrogant and of sinners. And His answer to them is no, your request is denied.

In Proverbs 1:24–31, God says, "Because I have called, and ye refused; I have stretched out my hand, and no man regarded; But ye have set at nought all my counsel, and would none of my reproof: I also will laugh at your calamity; I will mock when your fear cometh; When your fear cometh as desolation, and your destruction cometh as a whirlwind; when distress and anguish cometh upon you. Then shall they call upon me, but I will not answer; they shall seek me early, but they shall not find me: For that they hated knowledge, and did not choose the fear of the LORD: They would none of my counsel: they despised all my reproof. Therefore shall they eat of the fruit of their own way, and be filled with their own devices." By saying He will not answer, God is saying that His answer will be no. He will not grant the prayers of those who are not interested in doing His will. This is the silent answer of no.

In contrast to God's not hearing, David says in Psalm 6:9, "The LORD hath heard my supplication; the LORD will receive my prayer." In this verse, David is saying that God will *grant* his request. It is more accurate to say that God *grants* prayers than to say He *answers* prayers. It is a common mistake to say that God did not hear our prayer or did not answer our prayer, when what we should say is that He did not *grant* our prayer.

Who is responsible for prayers that do not get granted? God or you? Your answer will determine whether you are on the path to a great prayer life or a prayer life doomed to fail. God is predictable and unchanging. He does not fail. So responsibility must fall on you if your prayer life is failing to get the answers you want. God does not need to change, so you must. And if you are willing to change, He is willing to help you change.

THE ANSWERS TO FOUR TYPES OF PRAYERS

Recognizing God's answers to your prayers is easier than you might think. The key is to understand the four types of prayers. For each type of prayer, there will be an appropriate answer. If you know what answers to expect to each type of prayer, you can recognize God's answer for every prayer you offer. Those who serve God can expect the following answers to the four types of prayers:

1. Prayers for personal desires are requests either that you want to do or that you want God to do. The request is Can I..., or Will you...?

   - A definitive answer is revelation from God by faith, by His Word, or by godly counsel and will be a yes, a no, or a required condition to be fulfilled.

   - The Bible specifically says that persistence in prayer or prayer and fasting are sometimes required.

   - God may reveal some other requirement to different people. In John 9:7, Jesus required a blind man to wash his eyes with the water from the pool of Siloam.

   - Knowing the conditions requires listening to God, accepting His instructions, and obeying.

   - A silent answer to prayers for desires is a yes to the question, *Can I*. It is a no to the question, *Will you*.

2. Prayers for revelation are variations of prayers for desire. Your desire is that God reveal His answer to you, but you are not seeking a specific answer.

   - A definitive answer will be either the granting of your request, the denying of your request, or the revealing of a conditional requirement in order to be granted your request.

   - For example, deeper insight into God's truths is conditional based on God's requirement to learn and teach. Hebrews 6:3 says, "And this will we do, if God permit."

   - A silent answer to the request to know what God wants you to do leaves the choice up to you. For example, a silent answer to your request to know whether you should be a missionary in your neighborhood or in another country indicates that the choice is yours to make.

- A silent answer to the request to know what God will do for you is denial. For example, you might ask God to explain why all but one child died in a bus accident, and no explanation is given.

3. Prayers because of revelation are conditionally or unconditionally guaranteed.

- Conditional answers to prayers because of revelation require that you make your request, that you persist, that you fast, and/or that you do whatever else God requires of you. You contribute to change if you fulfill the required conditions.

- Unconditional answers will happen, whether you pray or not. For example, Jesus said to pray for His kingdom to come. It is definitely going to come, even if you do not pray for it to come. Because of these unconditional answers, some struggle with whether or not it is worth the bother to pray. But remember, prayers are for us, not for God. If He tells us to pray, then we should pray, whether the answer be conditional or unconditional.

4. Prayers because God answers are expressions of gratefulness, to which God responds by manifesting His love and approval.

Prayers for Desires:
Can I / Will You

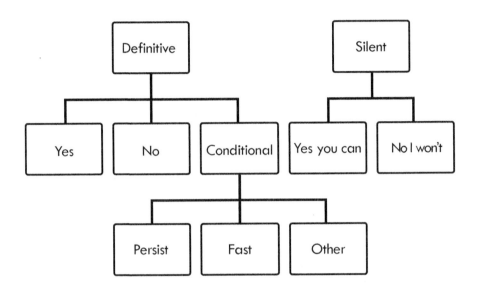

Understanding these four types of prayers helps us to see why we can expect God to answer every prayer and helps us to know how to recognize the meaning of every answer.

I offered all four types of prayers during my experience with cancer. When I was told that I had cancer, I began to ask God to show me how to pray. I offered *prayers for revelation*. Should I pray for my life, or should I pray that my death fulfill a good purpose to save souls? I spent a couple of weeks praying and waiting for an answer. Until God revealed to me that I could pray for my life, I was uncertain which choice I should make. The silent answer indicated that the choice was mine to make. So, I chose to continue asking Him to confirm what I should pray for. The choice to continue to pray was a *prayer of personal desire*. I wanted God to reveal to me what to do.

Understanding Prayers for Revelation: What, How, & Why

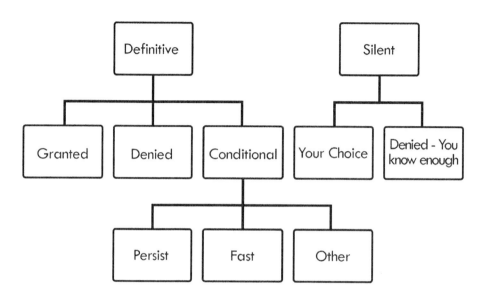

Being persistent resulted in receiving a definite answer from Him. It was only after I received a strong sense of God's permission to pray for my life that I began to ask Him to heal me. At that point, I offered *prayers because of revelation*. This was conditional permission, not a guarantee. The difference is that with permission, God would heal me if I believed and prayed. If I failed on my part to do so, then I would not have been healed. An unconditional guarantee would have resulted in my healing whether or not I believed and prayed.

I offered *prayers because God answers* to thank God for granting my prayers. He granted my prayers to know how He wanted me to pray. He granted my prayers of personal desire. He granted my prayers because of revelation. And He granted my request to learn about the prayers that move mountains.

SILENT ANSWERS

The disappointment we have with our prayers is that we want God to give us definite and unmistakable answers. We prefer to hear Him say *yes*. But even an undeniable *no* is thought to be better than no answer.

If we do not get the answer that we want the way we want it, then we are not happy with God's answer. This is not the right attitude for praying. The right way to pray is to trust Him to love us, to take care of us, and to answer every prayer with the best answers that will ultimately work together for good to all those who love Him.

First John 5:15 says, "… if we know that he hear us, whatsoever we ask, we know that we have the petitions that we desired of him." By God's Word and by faith, we know God hears our prayers, and we know He answers us. So then, what is the meaning of silent answers?

As I already said, when a verse says that God will not hear our prayers or that God did not answer our prayers, it is saying that God's answer is that He will not grant our requests. Silent answers from God can also have other meanings, depending on the type of prayer offered.

The meaning of a silent answer to *prayers for personal desires* depends on whether you are asking *God* to do something or you are asking Him to allow *you* to do something. A silent answer to your request for *God* to do something is a no, at least at the moment. Jesus said that we can persist in asking, so God's initial no could become a yes if we continue to ask. A silent answer to prayers for something *you* desire to do indicates that God does not disapprove, so you are permitted to do as you desire.

The meaning of a silent answer to *prayers for revelation* depends on whether the request is about something you could do or something only God could do. For example, if you are trying to decide what ministry to participate in, a silent answer would indicate that the choice is yours to make. In these cases, the *reason* for choosing is more important than the option chosen. First Corinthians 10:31 tells us that whatever we do, we should do everything for the glory of God.

You can always go the extra mile with persistence and fasting to make sure that you are making the right choice. But because you desire to serve God, if you make the wrong choice, God will correct you. He corrected Paul when he was planning to continue his ministry into Asia Minor. The Holy Spirit prevented him and sent him to Macedonia (Acts 16:6–9).

For *prayers because of revelation,* a silent answer indicates that you need to continue doing as you were told to do. You already know enough. How many times do you need to be told the same answer to the same question? How many times did Paul have to be told to preach the Gospel and to establish churches? How many times do you need to be told to live for God and to serve Him? How many times do you need to be told to pray for His kingdom to come? Some things never change, and so the answers never change and do not need to be repeated.

WHEN GOD'S ANSWERS ARE DELAYED

God answers prayers immediately. But we know from the prophet Daniel's experience that an answer can be delayed. God heard Daniel's prayer and answered immediately, but the answer was delayed because the messenger was engaged in a spiritual battle en route to Daniel. God could have made His answer known instantly if He wanted to. He could have revealed His answer personally. He had no need to use an angel as messenger. But He chose to use a messenger, and the answer was delayed. God knew it would be delayed. He deliberately allowed His answer to be delayed. Therefore, until the answer was made known, it was an immediate answer of silence, to be understood as a silent answer.

Why does God allow answers to be delayed? Undoubtedly, there are many reasons known only to God, and these include the reasons for God's silent answers mentioned previously. For example, the delay (silent answer) in responding to Mary and Martha's request that Jesus heal Lazarus was to emphasize the miraculous power of Christ.

Delayed answers are not due to neglect or inability on God's part. God is always in control. His plan includes delayed answers, which occur according to His design. His intent is to allow things to happen naturally and in consideration of the multitude of changes that are introduced because of choices made by angels and us. Every minute of our lives, we make decisions that change the course of history, if not for the world, then for ourselves and for those directly affected by us. The multitude of decisions we make for good or evil are calculated into how and when God answers our prayers. The point is that delayed answers, as in Daniel's case, are only delayed because God allows the delays.

Being in control does not mean God intervenes in every event detail that occurs in His creation. God has created the world to function by laws such as gravity, inertia, momentum, and thermodynamics. He is in control by allowing things to happen according to His design. These events are predictable. They are natural cause and effect events. Letting the rain fall on the good and the bad is the result of things occurring naturally according to the design of the world (Matthew 5:45). He controls all things by allowing the world to run its course naturally as He designed it.

By design, sin in the world naturally results in suffering and death. As bad as things are in the world, it would be a lot worse without God's intervention. In light of Daniel's experience, answers to prayers can be delayed due to interference by evil, but only if God allows it.

In some cases, God intervenes to change the natural course of events. These are miracles. Miraculous interventions do happen, but they are the exceptions to how things naturally happen in the world. He intervenes miraculously when it is required to fulfill His purpose of winning the maximum number of souls to Himself. A miraculous intervention that is easily overlooked because it is common is His restraint on evil. Without God's intervention to restrain evil, the world would be unlivable. Jesus described the result of unrestrained evil in Matthew 24:22, saying, "And except those days should be shortened, there should no flesh be saved...."

What should we do when God answers with silence or when an answer is delayed? Daniel continued to pray. Mary and Martha continued to pray. The Apostle Paul continued doing as the Holy Spirit originally directed him, and he single-mindedly continued to establish churches in Asia Minor. Paul was engaged in fulfilling God's will and being obedient to His calling. Paul did not change his course of ministry until the Lord told him to change. As I mentioned earlier, Acts 16:6 says that on one occasion Paul was "... forbidden of the Holy Ghost to preach the word in Asia." When God was ready to change the details of where Paul should serve, He made it clear. Only then did Paul change what he was doing. This is how to respond to silent answers. We should continue doing what God told us to do until He tells us to do differently.

Paul was content to do God's will, whatever the circumstances God allowed him to be in. He was content to continue doing what he was told to do. He did not pursue change. In Philippians 4:11, Paul says, "Not that I speak in respect of want: for I have learned, in whatsoever state I am, therewith to be content." Paul did not seek to change his circumstances. He just did as he was told. Any requests from Paul to God would have been about details to continue doing his job.

Is it wrong to ask for change? Not at all. As I explained earlier, God gives us permission to ask for the desires of our heart. We have permission to ask for whatever we want. It is up to us then to ask and to persevere in asking until He says yes or answers with a definitive no. Jesus says in Luke 18:1, "And he spake a parable unto them to this end, that men ought always to pray, and not to faint." The important thing is to be content with God's answer.

Obviously, it is wrong to complain. As we fulfill God's work to seek and to save the lost, we should be asking how to improve our skills and circumstances to do a better job of reaching more souls. If we are not content, our requests are not for God's will to be done but for our selfish desires.

How do you determine that you have waited long enough for God's answer? When should you stop praying for the same thing? If Daniel had to wait twenty-one days for the answer to his prayer for revelation, it should not surprise you that answers to your prayers may be delayed. But remember, God is in control. So it is up to God to make it clear to you that you should stop praying. Otherwise, keep praying and doing what you were originally told to do. This is what Jesus told us to do in Luke 18:1. Remember, He takes care of you if you are relying on Him and desiring to serve Him. God will tell you to stop making your request if He wants you to stop.

RECOGNIZING GOD'S ANSWERS

God is not the only one who gives answers to prayer requests. So how do you know if it is God's answer, Satan's answer, your answer, or someone else's answer?

If God is in control of your life, then you know that God is answering every prayer immediately. But can you distinguish between God's answer and other answers? If you are living your own life and fulfilling your own will, then you are not allowing

God to control your life. This makes you vulnerable to being misled by other influences. It will be difficult to know which answer is from God.

Here are seven important safeguards to help you discern God's answers to your prayers.

First, the only way to be confident in recognizing God's answers is to commit your life to Christ. When you are committed to Christ, you are able to apply the three prayer requirements of faith, belief, and righteousness. These are essential to having your prayers answered by God. *Faith* will help you understand His answers. *Belief* will be your acceptance of His answers. *Righteousness* will give you confidence that you have asked correctly and that you are able to recognize answers that are contrary to His Word.

Second, God's answers will never contradict His Word. If you are living right, then you are studying God's Word and learning about His will. You are learning how God thinks about things, and you will be increasing your ability to recognize God's answers.

Third, there is safety in the multitude of counselors. Receiving spiritual counsel is natural for those who are living right and participating in the church God has placed them in. Ephesians 4:14 says, "That we henceforth be no more children, tossed to and fro, and carried about with every wind of doctrine, by the sleight of men, and cunning craftiness, whereby they lie in wait to deceive." Godly counsel will not contradict God's Word. And remember, you will answer to God for doing what He told you to do. There is no one else to blame for your choices. Counsel is guidance, not a command. If a command is given in counsel, it should be a command that is verified from God's Word.

Fourth, over time, living for Christ, learning about God through Scriptures, and receiving counsel will lead to improved personal discernment by experience. You will learn from your mistakes and from your successes in recognizing answers that are from God.

Fifth, adjusting your expectations to match the answer that is appropriate for the type of prayer offered will help you recognize God's answer. As I have explained, there are four types of prayers. When you think all prayers should be granted the same way, there will be disappointment.

Sixth, recognizing the presence of evil will serve as a caution. Satan's counterfeit answers are going to create division between people, weaken God's work, and result in bad attitudes and feelings. First Corinthians 14:33 cautions that "... God is not the author of confusion, but of peace, as in all churches of the saints." Seek for clarity and a humble, calm spirit. Check the spirit influencing you. The Holy Spirit is always calm and compassionate.

Seventh, look for peace and comfort in your own heart. James 3:13–18 says, "Who is a wise man and endued with knowledge among you? let him shew out of a good conversation his works with meekness of wisdom. But if ye have bitter envying and strife in your hearts, glory not, and lie not against the truth. This wisdom descendeth not from above, but is earthly, sensual, devilish. For where envying and strife is, there is confusion and every evil work. But the wisdom that is from above is first pure, then peaceable, gentle, and easy to be intreated, full of mercy and good fruits, without partiality, and without hypocrisy. And the fruit of righteousness is sown in peace of them that make peace."

PRAY UNTIL YOU GET AN ANSWER

In Luke 18:1, Jesus exhorts us to continue making requests even when the answer is no, saying, "... that men ought always to pray, and not to faint." The parable in this passage is about a widow asking a judge for justice. Even though the judge did not grant her request initially, she persisted until he finally granted it. Jesus used this illustration to encourage us to always pray and not to quit. In fact, God not only gives us permission to persist in asking, but the widow's insistence encourages us to keep asking even when the answer is no.

The idea of persisting in prayer is interesting. God cannot be persuaded, informed, or coerced to do anything. The value of prayer to God is the pleasure of our fellowship and the pleasure He receives in granting our requests.

Prayer is for our benefit, and so God commands us to pray. When we pray right, our prayer life is satisfying and our requests are granted. If we do not pray right, then our prayers are not granted, and we struggle with a lack of desire to pray.

Ultimately, prayer is about our relationship with God. When our relationship with God is right, then we are praying right. Prayer without a relationship with God is an empty, meaningless exercise. It is not satisfying at all.

For those who do love God and pray right, requests still must be made before they are granted. This requirement makes us participants in God's work, and we are rewarded for doing well. And according to Luke 18:1, God holds back from granting some requests until we persist in asking. The requirement to persist builds character. It shows us that something really important to us is something worth praying for. Persistent prayer also reminds us of our dependence on God and results in a rewarding experience.

Persisting in making a request is not the same as ritualized repetitions. *Ritualistic* prayers are not about talking with God. They are about performing for God. They are religious formulas relying on method rather than on a relationship with God. Ritualized prayers could be said to a tree or a rock with the same response because the prayer is not about a loving relationship with God. It is about fulfilling a formula. Like the Pharisees praying in public for attention, those who offer ritualized prayers receive their reward, which in the Pharisees case was to fulfill a quota of repetitions. Jesus spoke of people praying this way in Matthew 6:7, saying, "But when ye pray, use not vain repetitions, as the heathen do: for they think that they shall be heard for their much speaking." God does not honor ritualistic repetitions.

The requirement for persistence suggests that there are prayer paths in our lives that are possible because of granted requests. I mentioned these paths earlier. To understand this idea, consider your life path without making any *prayers for personal desires* to be God's default path for your life.

There are two ways to deviate from this default path of God's will. You can deviate because of sin, or you can deviate because God grants a prayer request of yours. The *sin* paths occur because you have chosen to disobey God. The prayer paths are possible because God grants your requests for personal desires or lets you choose which paths to take.

Prayer paths fulfill God's will. So then, there is more than one path for your life that is in God's will. Proverbs 3: 5–6 says, "Trust in the LORD with all thine heart; and lean not unto thine own understanding. In all thy ways acknowledge him, and he shall direct thy paths." But to experience a particular path that God approves for your life requires that you ask. This makes prayer paths rewarding.

You may think that God has only one best path for your life. But the granting of prayers for your personal desires indicates that God allows for more than one path. If you do not make a request for a personal desire, then you do not receive it. This is not due to sin. You do not have to make requests for personal desires. And when God allows you to choose between two or more options, then obviously, God approves of all those paths.

The important thing to remember is that God gives you permission to persist in making your requests, even if He says no. When there is something that you really want, keep asking until He grants your request or tells you to stop asking.

Paul asked God three times to remove the thorn from his flesh. He asked the second time and third time because God told him no the first and second times. The third answer given must have been a definitive no, to stop asking. Or perhaps Paul decided his request was not worth the effort to persist. So he stopped asking. If God does not tell you to stop making a specific request, you have permission to keep asking as long as you feel it is important enough to do so. In the parable of the widow and the judge, Jesus put no limit on the number of times you can ask for something, even when the answer is no.

When I found out I had cancer, I prayed to know how God wanted me to pray. I asked God many times every day for two weeks to show me whether to pray for my life or not. I was not counting my requests or repeating a phrase over and over again as in ritualistic prayer. I was talking to God and asking Him for understanding. I kept asking Him until I had His answer.

WHEN GOD SAYS NO

When God says no, people wonder why. Some demand an explanation from God. But God owes no one an explanation. He answers to no one. We answer to God. It is up to us to trust Him, not to judge Him. His answers are the best answers, whether we understand why or not.

Nonetheless, it is not wrong to ask God why He does something. God wants us to understand. He wants us to pray for wisdom. He wants us to be blessed with insights and confidence. But demanding that God explain His answers is a form of complaint.

To understand God's will and why He says no, it is helpful to understand God's purpose for creation. Revelation 4:11 says, "... for thou hast created all things, and for thy pleasure they are and were created." God's pleasure is an infinite desire to bless. He created us because He loves us. He wants all of humanity to spend eternity with Him in fellowship, peace, and joy. First Timothy 2:4 says that God's will is for "... all men to be saved, and to come unto the knowledge of the truth." Nothing pleases God more than when people willingly respond to His gracious and loving promise to save them.

God's will is to bless, to love, and to do what is best for us. The more souls that are saved, the more God's will is fulfilled. Jesus said in Luke 19:10, "For the Son of man is come to seek and to save that which was lost." This is God's pleasure and goal. This is how to think about God's will and His answers to prayers. You may not see the immediate results you desire, but God sees the long term, ultimate goal desired. Those who desire God's will to be done trust Him. They know that His answers all work together for good to those who love Him.

God does not need to explain how and why His answers fulfill His will. Sometimes He does reveal details. Other times, He does not. Regardless of explanation, God's decisions always have in mind the salvation of souls. And His answers remain the best answers, with or without critique by us. They are the best answers, with or without our approval. What we need to do is believe that whatever He does works together for the good of those who love Him.

Those who trust God interpret everything with the perspective that God is in control, doing what is best to fulfill the goal of winning souls. If He says no to a request, then it is for the purpose of fulfilling His goal to save as many souls as possible. And those who trust Him rejoice in His answers.

When God says no, be thankful that He has given you the best answer. If possible, learn from your request and His answer. If you do not know something, ask. Ask God to teach you whether the answer no could have been avoided. Adjust your thinking and desires to conform to His way of thinking and desires.

Sometimes requests denied result in tragedy and sustained pain. This is life in a world ruled by Satan. What we learn from God's answers is how best to respond to such a world. Christ could have been delivered from torture and death, but He was not. King David's baby son could have been healed and given life, but he was not. The disciples could have been spared from suffering martyrdom, but they were not. God's people could have been protected from persecution and disease, but they were not. I have already explained why these things are allowed to happen, but explanations and understanding are irrelevant to whether God's answers to prayers are right and best. They are right and best regardless of what anyone thinks.

When God says no, be thankful. Trust Him. Don't be discouraged. Don't stop praying. Doing so is a protest against God's answers. But remember, if you don't like God's answers, then you are not praying with a desire for God's will to be done.

Instead of complaining about God's answers, we should consider complaining about our requests. Why did we not ask for something that God would say yes to? Why did we ask for something that was not according to God's will?

Does a perfect relationship with God result in knowing what to pray and what to expect? Does God always reveal everything to ask for to those praying by faith, believing in Him, and living righteously? Does a relationship with God eliminate ignorance and make every prayer offered a request that God will grant? The answer to these questions is no. A perfect relationship with God does not eliminate the limitations of our finite minds. We still have to ask Him for answers and understanding. This is how we learn.

This is God's will. If you are right with God, you will understand that there is nothing to complain about. You will trust Him.

WHEN GOD SAYS NO, NOT YET

There are many promises in the Bible already revealed that are not fulfilled yet. They will be, but not yet. For example, Jesus says in John 14:2, "In my Father's house are many mansions: if it were not so, I would have told you. I go to prepare a place for you." You can pray to live in your heavenly home, but it will not happen until the Lord says it is time for you to enter heaven.

Prayers for deliverance from suffering on the earth are common. Jesus says in John 16:20–22, "Verily, verily, I say unto you, That ye shall weep and lament, but the world shall rejoice: and ye shall be sorrowful, but your sorrow shall be turned into joy. A woman when she is in travail hath sorrow, because her hour is come: but as soon as she is delivered of the child, she remembereth no more the anguish, for joy that a man is born into the world. And ye now therefore have sorrow: but I will see you again, and your heart shall rejoice, and your joy no man taketh from you." The day is coming when Christ will establish His throne on Earth and eliminate Satan's presence. It is not yet, but it is coming. We can pray for His soon return, but up until this moment, the answer has been no, not yet.

How can the no, not yet answer be distinguished from the no answer? There is nothing to distinguish because the answer in both cases is no for the moment. Unless God reveals His promise to eventually say yes, there is no way to make the distinction between no and no, not yet.

Revelation of God's promises shows what God will do. But if God does not reveal whether the answer be no, not yet or a definite no, then it is important for us to continue making our request as though it is a no, not yet answer. This is the default perspective to have because Jesus said that we should not quit praying. This perspective keeps us praying at all times and all the time.

Some of my most memorable prayer experiences have been with the silent no, not yet answers when I asked God to teach me what a Bible verse means or to show me an answer to a question. One time I asked God to help me understand the difference between the Old Testament and the New Testament. I did not pray often, but the question would arise in my mind during studies, and I would make my request to understand. Then one day, I visited a student at his home off campus, and he asked me the question that I had been asking God. Suddenly, I knew the answer, and I shared it with the man. That experience and others have shown me that God uses time and experiences to teach us things.

I have asked Him why He does not download all the information and answers instantly into my mind. The understanding I have is that God rewards us for our efforts to grow in the knowledge of His truths. As Hebrews 6:3 says, "And this will we do, if God permit." It is a privilege to grow in the knowledge of God's truths, not a right. And the privilege to mature spiritually can be denied if we fail to obey God.

Does this make God mean or unloving? No, not at all. It is God's love for us that moves Him to do all that He does to save our souls and bless us with opportunities to serve Him. Giving us responsibility and rewards with accountability is not unloving. These are undeserved blessings. If there be any lack of love, it is on our part if we do not accept the responsibilities and seize the opportunities God graciously gives us.

GOD'S ANSWERS IN THE BIG PICTURE

Romans 8:28 says, "… all things work together for good to them that love God, to them who are the called according to his purpose." God knows all things. We do not. He knows how everything works from beginning to end. He sees all the dynamics of events and choices that people make from the foundation of the world to the end. He sees the trillions of events in every life throughout history, and He sees how every event triggers another event, which triggers another event and billions of events that follow after like a chain of dominoes through time. God alone knows what needs to happen now to maximize the number of saved souls in the future. If miraculous intervention be required, He will make it happen. If a request for a personal desire has no effect on the number of souls to be saved, then He may grant that request.

All things work together as guided and overseen by God for the ultimate good, the deliverance of souls from hell into heaven, the deliverance of souls from eternal death to eternal life. God answers every prayer with all things in mind to achieve the goal of winning the maximum number of souls.

We do not have such knowledge. We do not have the capacity to know such things. Because He has all things in mind, He knows what the best answer is for every prayer. We do not. For this reason, we should trust Him. He knows what He is doing.

God allowed Job to suffer at the hands of Satan. He allowed John the Baptist to sit in jail, followed by his execution by beheading. God allowed Paul to be hindered by the thorn in his flesh. He allowed His disciples and many others to be martyred. In the big picture of all things and in the course of trillions of events throughout history, God has answered prayers to maximize the number of souls who would be saved.

As I mentioned already, Mary and Martha asked Jesus to heal their brother, Lazarus. Jesus knew this family well. They were friends, and Jesus loved them. But He was in another town, and when the request reached Him, He delayed coming to them. He waited four days before coming in order to allow Lazarus to die.

There was grief and suffering. But Jesus was in control. In John 11:15, Jesus explained, "And I am glad for your sakes that I was not there, to the intent ye may believe; nevertheless let us go unto him." Jesus had a plan that Mary and Martha did not know. Rather than be distressed by Jesus' delay, they could have been comforted by the knowledge that Jesus was in control.

Some struggle with God's answers when they are denied their requests, especially for deliverance from evil. Some complain about God's allowing suffering and evil. But in the big picture, these are temporary problems, although they are oftentimes excruciating. God plans to bring sin and suffering to a complete end. Revelation 21:4 says of that time, "And God shall wipe away all tears from their eyes; and there shall be no more death, neither sorrow, nor crying, neither shall there be any more pain: for the former things are passed away." In fact, the future is incomparably better than all the current sufferings. Paul says in Romans 8:18, "For I reckon that the sufferings of this present time are not worthy to be compared with the glory which shall be revealed in us."

But in the meantime, God is allowing sin to run its course. And the negative effects of sin are predictable because of the design of creation. God will grant the prayers for His kingdom to come, but not yet. For now, He is delaying His coming in order to win as many souls as possible.

Our lack of understanding of what God is doing does not change God's plans. Our believing or not believing in Him does not change His plans. Whether we trust Him or not does not change His plans. But our trust in Him does make a difference in our plans and how we feel about things.

If we believe that God is in control, it is of little concern to us whether we understand what God's plan is or not. It is sufficient to know that God is in control. He sees the big picture from one end of eternity to the other. He sees the history of mankind on

Earth from generation to generation. He sees the beginning of all things, and He sees the end of all things. We, on the other hand, see only a small window of time in a small view of the world around us. We barely understand a hint of what we see and know. Relative to God, we know and understand nothing. Relative to the infinite knowledge of God's omniscience, we know nothing. Regardless of how much we learn and know, compared to infinite knowledge, it will always be nothing. Thus, our understanding of how things are and our explanations and expectations of what we would like God to do are founded in ignorance. We are not qualified to judge God or to question His plan. It is sufficient to know that He loves us and that He is in control. And what He does reveal to us is very gracious on His part.

During Job's trial of suffering, he and his friends wondered what was wrong with him. Why was God allowing him to be cursed? God made it clear to him that the explanation was not important. What was important was that Job accepted God's will despite the circumstances. God does not have to justify His will to us. He does not have to explain. He made the stars, and He created the world without our help or critique, and He will continue to do things without having to justify His ways to us. It is we who must seek to be justified in His eyes. And because we cannot justify ourselves, we must rely on Him with complete dependence. This is especially true when circumstances are not good for us.

If God allowed Satan to harass Job, is it not possible that you too may have been chosen to fulfill a role such as Job did in his time? If God required Paul to minister with the thorn in his flesh, then why should we expect more comfort and less hindrance? We serve God, not because of the walls He puts around us and the favors He bestows on us; we serve Him because He is worthy to be served. He is God. He is our Creator. When Job faced the loss of everything but his life, he fell on his face and worshipped God. He did not challenge or blame God. We should not complain about

His will either, and we will not complain if we trust Him and accept His answers as the best answers.

We must look to God, not our circumstances, to know what to do. We must be controlled by God, not our circumstances, to fulfill His plans for our lives. We must delight in the Lord, not in our circumstances. We must delight in the Lord, not in ourselves. We must delight in the Lord, not in our requests. We must delight in the Lord's will, not in ours.

God's big plan includes all the options with one goal in mind, to save souls. This is the big picture. God desires to save all souls. But His plan is to allow every person to make his or her own choice. Second Peter 3:9 says, "The Lord is not slack concerning his promise, as some men count slackness; but is longsuffering to us-ward, not willing that any should perish, but that all should come to repentance." And First Timothy 2:3–4 says, "For this is good and acceptable in the sight of God our Saviour; Who will have all men to be saved, and to come unto the knowledge of the truth."

God does not condemn souls to hell because He gets pleasure in doing so. He made this abundantly clear by dying for our sins and making salvation possible. Souls are condemned to hell because of the necessity for justice and righteousness. He wants to establish a perfect heaven and earth where there is no sin. Second Peter 3:13–14 says, "Nevertheless we, according to his promise, look for new heavens and a new earth, wherein dwelleth righteousness. Wherefore, beloved, seeing that ye look for such things, be diligent that ye may be found of him in peace, without spot, and blameless." The coming new heaven and new earth will be a holy place without sin. When sin is eliminated, suffering and death will be eliminated. This is what God wants.

The elimination of suffering and death can only happen when sin is eliminated. And this requires that every person, according to Second Peter 3:14, be "found of him in peace, without spot, and blameless." This means to be at peace with God, not at odds with Him and not facing condemnation. This requires being without sin. If heaven is to be sinless, then those who live in heaven must be sinless, without spot of contamination, and blameless of sin.

I know that sounds impossible. It sounds impossible because it is impossible. No one can claim to be sinless. No one. All are born sinners with a sin nature. So then how do people get into heaven? Only by the mercy and grace of God. He must miraculously make you sinless. And that is His plan. He is not going to force this on you. He requires that you believe in Him. He requires that you really want this change (repentance) and that you will permit Him to change you (new birth).

In Matthew 23:37, Jesus expressed His desire for Israel, their choice, and His predictable response all according to His plan, saying, "O Jerusalem, Jerusalem, thou that killest the prophets, and stonest them which are sent unto thee, how often would I have gathered thy children together, even as a hen gathereth her chickens under her wings, and ye would not!" God desired to bless Israel. Israel's choice was to reject Him. And God's response was to deny them blessings they could have had.

God's plan is to establish a kingdom of righteousness. His will is that everyone be included. But His plan is to let everyone make the choice individually. It is the choice to obey or to disobey God that determines the destination of one's life path.

For those who reject His offer, sin and the consequences that come with it are their choice. With sin come pain, misery, suffering, and death. This is not God's desire for people, but it is His plan should they choose sin over Him. God cannot allow sin in heaven, or it would be corrupted with pain and death too. We already have that here on Earth. Heaven is the opportunity for us to live without sin and suffering.

SAYING THANK YOU

When you make a request of God, tell Him thank you. He has already answered your prayer. Many people make requests and forget about them or complain when they do not receive what they ask for. After Jesus healed ten men suffering from leprosy, only one thanked Him (Luke 17:15–16). How many thank God today for all the blessings enjoyed?

We have much to be thankful for, including that He is in control of all things, that He loves us, that He answers every prayer, and that His answers are always the best answers. He allows us to breathe His air, to walk on His earth, to enjoy the warmth of His sun, to explore His creation to gain wonderful insights, and to have the ability to reverse engineer His ingenious creations into useful tools.

Prayers because God answered are prayers of gratefulness. Luke 2:25–30 describes how a prophet thanked God because of being granted a prayer for revelation. "And, behold, there was a man in Jerusalem, whose name was Simeon; and the same man was just and devout, waiting for the consolation of Israel: and the Holy Ghost was upon him. And it was revealed unto him by the Holy Ghost, that he should not see death, before he had seen the Lord's Christ. And he came by the Spirit into the temple: and when the parents brought in the child Jesus, to do for him after the custom of the law, Then took he him up in his arms, and blessed God, and said, Lord, now lettest thou thy servant depart in peace, according to thy word: For mine eyes have seen thy salvation."

Regardless of God's answer, thank Him for giving you the best answer. Thank Him for answering your prayer. Say thank you for the yes, the no, and the no, not yet answers. Thank Him for the revealed answers and the silent answers. Be grateful that His will was done. Thank Him when you are given the responsibility to choose from options. Thank Him that you are permitted to offer your requests. Accept His answers, and don't complain.

Knowing God always does what is best for saving the maximum number of souls is essential to understanding God's answers to prayers. Regardless of the answers to our prayers, we can thank God for His love for us and trust Him to do what is best. And when I say what is best, I am not saying that it is always without suffering. Suffering is part of living in a sin-corrupted world.

As I mentioned earlier, our choices to sin are the causes of suffering. The world we live in reminds us what a world without God would be like. God is not responsible. God allows us to experience the consequences of choosing to do things our own way. The consequences include minimizing His role in protecting us. The reason that we receive any blessings at all is His love for us. But when we choose to sin, we are telling Him that we prefer our ways rather than His. And how is that working out for us?

Babies die of cancer; hurricanes destroy properties, causing loss and suffering; malicious thugs rape and kill; famines and pestilences cause prolonged misery and death. This is not the world God created for us. This is a world we chose when we chose sin. When we choose sin, we are telling God to back off and let us do things our way. So He distances Himself. And what do we do when our way ends up causing suffering? We complain that He doesn't care about us.

The more rational response would be to tell God that we are sorry, that we are wrong, that His ways are better than ours, and that we need Him. Admitting God is right is the better way. Suffering the consequences of a world plagued by sin is the best way to help us realize that we are wrong. Can you imagine what those who still think their way is better than God's, even in a world suffering from sin, would say if there was no suffering? More than likely, they would convince themselves that they have no need for God because there is no suffering. Those who do not want to believe in God will always find an excuse to justify their opinion.

God does protect most from the worst of evil. A world without the protection of God would be a world of indescribable horror and pain for everyone. All of life would be annihilated. Referring to the end days when God turns the earth over to Satan, Jesus said in Matthew 24:22 that "… except those days should be shortened, there should no flesh be saved: but for the elect's sake those days shall be shortened." Evil unrestrained by God would have ended the world long ago.

Because we live in a world corrupted by sin right now, it is important to remember that God's answers to our individual prayers involve more than us individually. He sees the big picture. He knows the future paths and the choices being made by all people. He knows which answers to our prayers are best for everyone and for all those affected now and into the future.

God's answers might involve depriving us. They might involve personal suffering, but not because He desires for us to suffer. As I explained before, God's answers are all done in the context of what brings about the greatest good for everyone in a world of sin. A baby suffering from cancer reminds us that we do not want to live in a world of sin without God. Suffering inflicted on us by evil people reminds us that we need God's protection.

In my case, suffering from cancer was not what I wanted or expected, but the experience taught me a lot about prayer. It was a part of the answer to my prayer to understand more about prayer. It is one thing to talk about prayer that moves mountains or to hear others talk about it, but it is another to experience it firsthand. I prayed to understand the prayers that move mountains, and God gave me a mountain to move.

In a perfect world, God's answers would never involve suffering. But we live in an imperfect world corrupted by sin and ruled by Satan. This is not God's fault. This is our fault. We choose to sin and to do things our way every day. God warns that sin causes misery and death. But we go ahead and sin anyway. So then, God weaves answers into our sinful lives to ultimately lead us to make the right choices and to seek a perfect life with Christ in heaven. But until then, we need to trust God to know and to do what is best and to accept His answers as the best answers.

There are those who say God should make the world perfect without suffering if He is a loving God. But this is another example of arrogant humanity insisting their way is better than God's. They want sin and disobedience without the consequences. They want to use God like a Genie in a lamp. They want to tell God what to do and how to do it. They insult God by choosing sin and rejecting His instructions and then expect Him to protect them from the harm that comes with their decisions. He already allows us to live, to breathe His air, to walk on His soil, to enjoy His sunshine, and much more. And in spite of being rejected, He does offer some protection from evil and its consequences. These things are more than we deserve. He blesses us in spite of ourselves. Remember, things could be a lot worse.

Most importantly, he does not abandon us. He is always ready to forgive us and is eager to give us the hope and promise of eternal life in heavenly bliss. Why? He loves us. He wants only the best for us. And this is the reason He answers every prayer with only the best answers.

GREAT INSIGHTS TO REMEMBER

1. Desiring God's will guarantees that every prayer will be granted.

2. The problem is not God's failure to answer prayers; it is our failure to accept His answers.

3. I believe in prayer because I believe in God.

4. When God has your heart, your prayers are granted.

5. God will answer the prayer to know what is wrong with the way you pray.

6. The power of prayer is not in our words, but in Him who hears our words. The power of prayer is not in the one praying, but in the one answering. The power of prayer is not in the will of man, but in the will of God.

7. When you delight in the Lord, every answer from God is the desire of your heart.

8. God answers every prayer immediately with the appropriate answer according to His will.

9. If we do not ask, then we may not receive what could have been a blessing in our lives.

10. The question to ask is not whether God answers prayers. Rather, it is to ask *how* to pray prayers that God will grant.

11. We need to trust God that He is in control, that He answers every prayer, that every answer is the best answer, and that all things work together for good to them that love God.

12. What we call unanswered prayers are really answered prayers.

13. Even a delayed answer is a deliberate answer.

14. "Unanswered" prayers are silent answers from God.

15. When we pray right, our prayer life is satisfying, and our requests are granted.

16. Prayer is about our relationship with God.

17. God gives you permission to persist in making your requests even when He says no.

18. God's answers are the best answers, whether we understand why or not.

19. When you make a request of God, tell Him thank you.

6
PRAYERS OF HOPE

Rejoicing in hope; patient in tribulation;
continuing instant in prayer.
—Romans 12:12

Hope is optimistic expectation that something desired will happen. People hope for many good things to happen to them that may or may not happen. But hope in God's promises is not wishful expectation that something *might* happen. It is expectation *without a doubt* that God will fulfill His promises.

Our expectation that God will fulfill His promises is founded on His power and integrity. Hebrews 6:17–18 says that we have absolute confidence and hope in God because His counsel (purpose, will) is immutable and because His promise to His heirs is sealed with His oath. He cannot lie, so His promise of eternal life to those who believe in Him is guaranteed. Nothing can change His promise, and nothing can prevent it.

For many, the question is not whether God *can* do something. The question is *will* God do something. Hope in God's promises is a hope that has no doubt that God can and will do something. We can desire that God do something and wish that He would. But hope without doubt is based on believing that God will fulfill His will and promise.

I had hope in God's ability to heal me of my cancer for good reason. Nothing is impossible for God. He created the universe in seven days, so healing me would not pose any difficulty. There was no doubt that God *could* heal me.

I had no doubt that God was able to heal me. The question was would He heal me?

The questions I struggled with for two weeks after being told that I had cancer were would God use His power to heal me and did He want to heal me? I had no doubt that God was able to heal me. The question was would He heal me? Once God gave me permission to pray for my healing, I prayed with hope to be healed. I relaxed. I was at peace. I was in God's hands.

God confirmed in me by faith that He was answering my prayer to understand prayers that move mountains. I also had confirmation from those who were close to God.

Whether I lived or died, I would be in God's hands. I was hopeful in Christ. Paul expressed his hope in Christ in Philippians 1:21, saying, "For to me to live is Christ, and to die is gain." Living or dying is all about Christ. The hope for living now in this physical world is that God is in control and answers every prayer. The hope in death is to live in heaven forever. Whether believers live or die, they have reason to be hopeful. Their hope is in Christ.

Paul shared an interesting perspective about living. In Galatians 2:20, he said, "I am crucified with Christ: nevertheless I live; yet not I, but Christ liveth in me: and the life which I now live in the flesh I live by the faith of the Son of God, who loved me, and gave himself for me." Paul found fulfillment and contentment by living for Christ. He surrendered himself and all that he did to Christ. Living this way would make it impossible to be hopeless. Christ was in control, and everything that happened to Paul was according to God's will.

I knew that medically the odds of survival were against me, especially when the cancer reoccurred. But my hope was in Christ. I knew that His will would be done. That made me hopeful.

Regardless of the medical advances and successes, your hope should always be in Christ. God made man intelligent. And man has used His God-given mind to solve many problems. But the abilities of man are still finite, imperfect, and not guaranteed to succeed 100 percent. Unlike God, man is *not* infallible or all-powerful. The many accomplishments of mankind are incomparable to all that God has done. Mankind can explore, learn, and apply knowledge gained from God's creation. But God alone designed and created all things. Your hope should be in Him. When you pray for healing, also pray for the doctors and the nurses. They need all the help they can get. They can apply knowledge gained from studying creation, but they are still dependent on God for their skills and their own health.

Everyone dies at some point. Isaiah 64:6 says, "But we are all as an unclean thing, and all our righteousnesses are as filthy rags; and we all do fade as a leaf; and our iniquities, like the wind, have taken us away." There is no medical cure to heal a dead body. No one possesses a physical body that will live forever. Isaiah 40:7 says, "The grass withereth, the flower fadeth: because the spirit of the LORD bloweth upon it: surely the people is grass."

I was healed over thirty years ago, but someday I most certainly will die, just like everyone else. I am still vulnerable to diseases and aging. My healing was a lesson at one point in time in my life. It was a part of God's answer to my request. But that healing will not prevent my death from ever occurring. Does that sound hopeless? Not at all. My hope is in God's promise. He saved me, and someday He will give me a new body that will never die. Everyone who trusts in Jesus Christ has the same hope.

Hope follows belief and trust. If you trust Christ, you will be absolutely hopeful. This kind of hope is rooted in Christ, not in people. Christ loves us, though we are sinners. Christ cannot be prevented from saving those who trust Him. Christ cannot fail to deliver on His promise to give eternal life. Paul wrote in First Timothy 1:1 about his hope in Christ and his calling as an apostle, saying it was by "… the commandment of God our Saviour, and Lord Jesus Christ, which is our hope." Jesus Christ is the reason for hope of anything that is good.

> *Christ cannot fail to deliver on His promise to give eternal life.*

There is always hope in Christ. Though the world is on a course leading to destruction, those in Christ look forward to living in a new heaven and earth (Second Peter 3:13) that will never corrupt. Christ promised to return physically to Earth and to redeem everyone who believes Him. Nothing can prevent Him. He will fulfill His promise. In Him, all believers have hope without doubt. There is hope in the promises of God now and for later. There is hope of having your life used by God. There is hope of salvation, regardless of what happens now. There is hope of eternal fellowship with God. There is hope of eternal peace with Christ. Titus 2:13 says we should be "Looking for that blessed hope, and the glorious appearing of the great God and our Saviour Jesus Christ."

PRAYERS OF HOPE

If you understand prayer, you will always have hope. There are no formulas or scripted prayers from which to gain hope. Prayers of hope are prayers that come from your heart. They are the result of your trust in God, not in your words. They are your desires expressed along with the desire for God's will to be done, not as rituals to oblige God to grant your request. They are prayers to make things better. They are prayers with optimistic expectations to improve circumstances. They are prayers of confidence that God will grant your requests because of your love for Him.

Prayers of hope are prayers that come from your heart. They are the result of your trust in God, not in your words.

The most important prayer of hope is the prayer of salvation. There is not a script or special words to say. It is simply confessing to God that you believe in Him. Romans 10:9 says, "That if thou shalt confess with thy mouth the Lord Jesus, and shalt believe in thine heart that God hath raised him from the dead, thou shalt be saved." This is not about confessing audibly with your voice special words to other people. The *confession* in this verse takes place the moment you believe. It occurs at the moment you realize the truth of God. This is a confession to God of dependence on Him because you believe He is the only One who can save you.

When you believe God's Word that you are a sinner facing eternal condemnation, that Jesus died to pay for your sins, that God raised Him from the dead, that you must rely on Him alone to qualify you for heaven, and that He can and wants to give you eternal life, you are saved. When you believe, your acceptance of Him and of His Word is your prayer. This is a prayer

If you are looking for hope, your salvation is the first thing to take care of.

to God of realization that you believe. This is the moment you meet Him and agree with Him. It is a personal encounter based on recognizing and accepting Him as your God. This means that you are saved at the moment you believe. Jesus says in John 5:24, "Verily, verily, I say unto you, He that heareth my word, and believeth on him that sent me, hath everlasting life, and shall not come into condemnation; but is passed from death unto life." You are now on speaking terms. His presence is real and personal to you. You are saved and have eternal life. This is guaranteed by God's promise. If you are looking for hope, your salvation is the first thing to take care of.

Another prayer of hope is for the abundant life. Jesus says in John 10:10, "... I am come that they might have life, and that they might have it more abundantly." In addition to eternal life, Jesus came to give an abundant life, which occurs the moment you believe. Eternal life is abundant life because it is forever. But *abundance* includes the meaning of an extraordinary, better, and more meaningful life. Christians have a higher purpose for living than prior to their salvation. They are called to be the children and representatives of God, the Creator of all things. Christians are given a mission to proclaim His message and are given the role of training others to do likewise. Second Corinthians 5:17 says, "Therefore if any man be in Christ, he is a new creature: old things are passed away; behold, all things are become new." There is nothing more extraordinary and amazing than to serve the Creator of all things. Christians live for something much greater than themselves and much greater than anything else in the world.

In First John 5:14–15, the Apostle John says we have hope that our prayers will be granted, saying, "And this is the confidence that we have in him, that, if we ask any thing according to his will, he heareth us: And if we know that he hear us, whatsoever we ask, we know that we have the petitions that we desired of him." Remember, God answers every prayer. And with the right perspective, you can rejoice in every answer, knowing that God only gives answers that will lead to the maximum number of souls saved. This makes every answer the best answer possible. To guarantee that your prayers will be granted, you must pray in accordance with God's will by faith in God, believe God, pray right, and apply the appropriate effort (persistence and fasting) if required.

With the right perspective, you can rejoice in every answer, knowing that God only gives answers that will lead to the maximum number of souls saved.

Feeling pessimistic? Feeling depressed about your circumstances? Feeling weary of difficulties in your life? Pray to be hopeful. Ask God to remind you of all the things to be thankful for, especially of His promises that are guaranteed. Try letting God tell you what to pray for and what to expect, rather than telling Him what you want and what you expect from Him. If God reveals that He is permitting you to pray for something, rejoice, pray, and be thankful for His promise and permission. This will give you hope.

Things to pray for:

- Pray for everything.
- Pray hopefully for your health.
- Pray hopefully for your marriage.
- Pray hopefully for your children.
- Pray hopefully for your family and friends.
- Pray hopefully for your daily needs.
- Pray hopefully for your deliverance from evil.

- Pray hopefully for a purposeful life.
- Pray hopefully for your church and ministry.
- Pray hopefully for Christ's return and His kingdom on Earth.
- Pray hopefully for forgiveness.
- Pray hopefully for you to do God's will.
- Pray hopefully for your wisdom.
- Pray hopefully to help others.

If you are wondering how to pray hopefully for any of these things, ask God. Ask God what you should pray for. Rely on Him to guide you in your prayers. It is time to practice what you have learned.

Remember prayer is for you. It is not for God. You can ask for whatever you want. And God will give you the best answer. Be thankful for God's answer. He knows what He is doing. This is a good reason to be hopeful.

PERSECUTION AND HARDSHIP

You may be discouraged. You may be hurting. You may be persecuted. You may be dying. But these things cannot defeat you as long as you trust God and believe He will fulfill His promises. Psalm 34:19 reminds us that "Many are the afflictions of the righteous: but the LORD delivereth him out of them all." Regardless of the harm done to you or the influence to hinder your testimony, no one can take away God's promise from you, or your hope in Christ, or your freedom to choose to honor God. Your choice is the one thing no one can touch. Always choose to remain faithful to God no matter what. He will always be faithful to you.

In Romans 5:1–4, Paul explains why we can hope in God,

regardless of the trials we might experience. He says, "Therefore being justified by faith, we have peace with God through our Lord Jesus Christ: By whom also we have access by faith into this grace wherein we stand, and rejoice in hope of the glory of God. And not only so, but we glory in tribulations also: knowing that tribulation worketh patience; And patience, experience; and experience, hope." In other words, our hope (absolute, optimistic expectation) that God will fulfill His promise to give us abundant life forever is confirmed by our experiences with tribulations. Those who trust God experience His personal assurance by faith that all will be well. In tribulations, God comforts and gives strength. This personal experience with God is reassuring. It enables us to endure tribulations for the moment while looking forward to the fulfillment of God's promises that all tribulations will one day cease forever.

Hebrews 11:1 says that faith is the *substance of things hoped for*. He further states that faith is *evidence of things not seen*. What is this evidence upon which we base our hope in Him? It is the revelation from God of His personal assurance and confirmation that His Word is true. This evidence (faith) is given to us directly from God to convince us of things that cannot be seen or confirmed in the physical world. Faith (revelation from God) is the reason we understand and believe in God and His promises. Faith is the evidence that we believe. Faith is the substance of what we hope for because it is personalized revelation from God to us. There is no greater assurance of things to hope for than God's promises revealed to us.

Hope is based on the unbreakable, guaranteed promise of God.

We have hope in God because He has given us a reason to believe. He gives us revelation of His promises. He reveals to us His assurance that He will do what He promised. This means that faith serves as the foundation upon which our hope in God is based. We hope in God because He reveals His personal guarantee that He will do what He promises. His promise revealed makes it possible for us to have hope and subsequently have peace with God. Hope is based on the unbreakable, guaranteed promise of God.

The *glory* of God Paul speaks of in this passage is God's approval and acceptance of those who are justified in His eyes, those who believe in Him. Believers know with certainty by faith that God has justified them and has accepted them with full approval. This is the hope believers have in God and rejoice about. Being justified by God means believers are at peace with God.

Paul says that believers rejoice in tribulations because tribulation produces patience, patience in turn produces experience, and experience in turn produces hope. In other words, hardships can serve as sources of hope. This is a different way of thinking about hard times in life.

Paul is not saying that we look forward to difficulties. Rather, because trials are inevitable in a world of sin, trials remind us of the promise God has given to deliver us. Trials in this life, no matter how horrible, are temporary. But through every trial, God reassures us of His love for us and His promise to deliver us to eternal blessings.

> *Because trials are inevitable in a world of sin, trials remind us of the promise God has given to deliver us.*

Tribulations remind us of what we are being delivered from. Sin in the world produces the fruit of hate, violence, and suffering. Sin is the cause of condemnation. Sin is the cause of tribulations. We accept the fact that there are consequences in a sin-plagued world. But rather than despair when we suffer the consequences of sin, believers can rejoice in the hope of Christ's promises to deliver us from sin and suffering.

Believers overcome tribulation by drawing closer to God. Rather than allow tribulations to discourage us, we can use them to experience His presence and help. Tribulations do not make us happy, but we must accept them as inevitable in a world of sin. In First Corinthians 10:13, Paul reminds us that "There hath no temptation taken you but such as is common to man: but God is faithful, who will not suffer you to be tempted above that ye are able; but will with the temptation also make a way to escape, that ye may be able to bear it." We all share in the miseries of a sin-filled world. Some suffer more than others. But everyone has access to God's comforting presence. All we have to do is believe in Him.

Paul writes about his personal experience dealing with suffering and fear in Second Corinthians 7:4–6, saying, "… I am filled with comfort, I am exceeding joyful in all our tribulation. For, when we were come into Macedonia, our flesh had no rest, but we were troubled on every side; without were fightings, within were fears. Nevertheless God, that comforteth those that are cast down, comforted us by the coming of Titus." Though we suffer in tribulations, God offers comfort. And the experience of His comfort reminds us of the ultimate comfort we hope for once He delivers us from this world of sin.

God loves you, and He wants you to be hopeful in Him. There is comfort in hope because God assures you that He will do what He promises. And with His guarantee to save your soul, if you believe in Him, you will be comforted.

OVERCOMING HOPELESSNESS

Many people pray when tragedy strikes. In fact, one survey reported that twenty percent of those who feel that God's existence is unlikely pray just to *feel* safer. The idea of God being there, hearing us, and being able to do something about our circumstances drives us to pray. There is something in us that provokes us to cry out to God in times of trouble. It is by design. God designed us to need Him. And when we are in trouble, we instinctively call out to Him.

Romans 1:20–21 affirms that we know God or at least did know Him. "For the invisible things of him from the creation of the world are clearly seen, being understood by the things that are made, even his eternal power and Godhead; so that they are without excuse: Because that, when they knew God, they glorified him not as God, neither were thankful; but became vain in their imaginations, and their foolish heart was darkened."

God reveals Himself to us personally and through creation. By personalized, internal revelation (faith), He confirms His presence, His righteousness, and His wrath against unrighteousness. By creation, He reveals Himself in the physical design and the laws of nature.

God is the intelligent Creator of all things. He has the blueprints on how things work. He is the source of information needed to know how to live in His world. If you want to know how to live to your fullest potential, you need to follow His instructions.

Many dismiss God as unimportant. Many take the blessings of God for granted and do not appreciate the life He has given to us nor His offer of a blessed and perfect future. Once God is rejected, then people invent explanations about our origins and about how to live. This is substituting truth with whimsical imaginations.

Substituting truth with fake narratives leads to problems. It is bad enough living in a world of sin. But making decisions based on wrong ideas about God and His creation compounds the problems. This leads to hopelessness.

Job 27:8 says, "For what is the hope of the hypocrite, though he hath gained, when God taketh away his soul?" It is hypocritical to think that we do not need God because we are doing well. Health, wealth, talent, and fame might make you feel justified in what you do and how you think about God, but these do not justify you. Being right with God is the only way to be justified, regardless of your circumstances.

It is also hypocritical to pray to God when we deny His importance and then complain about the results. It makes no sense to blame God for all that is wrong in the world and then to ask Him for help. It makes no sense to insult God by denying His existence and then ask Him to heal you. It seems more logical that those who have had

It makes no sense to insult God by denying His existence and then ask Him to heal you.

no need for God would have no need for prayer. But tragedy has a way of forcing people to admit their wrongs.

Hardships and afflictions make many feel out of control and defeated. Some even question whether God is really in control or loving. But He is. Regardless of what His enemies do, being on God's side is always the right side. God's enemies may use your difficult circumstances to challenge the claim that God is loving and kind, but remember, your life is small in the context of what God sees. God sees your life in the context of all life on Earth and in the timeline of history and the future. Though such a big picture could make one feel insignificant, to God every soul receives His infinite attention and care.

The death of Christ on the cross is a good example of what appeared to be a defeat for Christ. But this was actually a victory. The wages of sin is death, and by dying for us, Christ was paying for our freedom from the curse of sin. It was the only way to pay for our sins. It was excruciatingly, infinitely painful. It looked like defeat, but it was actually victory.

Death and suffering are constant reminders that sin brings pain and sorrow. Death and suffering remind us that the consequences of sin are painful, and that sin will defeat us. There is nothing good or pleasant about the consequences of sin. So when bad things or unpleasant things happen, just remember, sin is the cause of suffering and death. And the experiences of suffering and death are to be expected in a sin-plagued world.

Nonetheless, there is hope in our world. Jesus shares His victory over sin and death. This is the message of hope God wants everyone to hear. In Christ, there is an end to failure, and sin is defeated. Our testimonies as believers should give others reason to hope in Jesus Christ.

Job is a good example of holding on to hope in God despite suffering. Job tragically lost his children and possessions, yet Job 1:22 says, "In all this Job sinned not, nor charged God foolishly." Whereas many are quick to blame God for allowing troubles to come into their lives, Job understood that God was not responsible. Job knew that ultimately sin was the cause of suffering in the world.

Job's story is one of remaining faithful to God and not giving up on hope in God's promises despite the experience of suffering. In spite of all that Job suffered, he worshipped God and did not sin. This means that Job did not blame God for his suffering. What a powerful testimony! What fortitude! What character! Satan took everything from Job but his life, and yet Job remained faithful to God. Even when Job's closest friends challenged his integrity, Job remained faithful.

Why did Job suffer? What was the cause of his suffering if it did not come from God? His friends mistakenly concluded that a man's circumstances are indicative of a man's sins. As many do today, Job's friends believed that comfort and ease in life were an indication of being right with God. They mistakenly thought calamity and suffering in life were indications of being wicked and being cursed for sinning.

Job's wealth, health, family, friends, and reputation were taken from him. Because of the wrong perspective of his friends, Job was accused of hidden sin. Job could not defend himself. The evidence of misery in his life justified the erroneous thinking that he was wicked. Job knew better, but he could not persuade his friends.

Fortunately, Job chose to remain faithful to God in spite of his personal misery and in spite of what his friends said about him. God was worthy of honor and gratefulness, regardless of Job's circumstances.

Circumstances change, but God never does. Job was searching for answers and trying to make sense out of his circumstances. God pointed out that He was in control, whether or not Job understood. God does not have to justify Himself to men. God does not have to take man's sorrows away to prove His compassion. God does not have to be explainable. God does not have to be understood. God does not have to answer to man. Man answers to God. We need Him. He does not need us.

God does not have to take man's sorrows away to prove His compassion.

The fact is that God has demonstrated His love for us by sacrificing Himself to pay for our sins. This was an eternal payment. He did not need to do this for Himself. It was 100 percent grace on His part to voluntarily suffer the excruciating, infinite pain. His suffering was beyond comprehension. If He did nothing more than give us eternal life, He would have given us infinitely more than we deserve. It is unimaginable to think that people would demand more of God or blame Him for their suffering.

God does not have to answer to man. Man answers to God.

An interesting lesson that is often overlooked in Job's story is why God is worthy of honor even though we suffer. Just as Job could not defend himself to those blinded by superficial, faulty thinking, God cannot defend Himself in the eyes of those who have faulty thinking and who are unwilling to credit Him for goodness because of the suffering in the world. Fools accuse God because He does not do things the way they think He should do things. Job, however, did not follow the example of others. He did not accuse God, even though he struggled with his lack of understanding.

The issue most people struggle with is not whether God is in control, nor is it that bad things happen in life. The issue is *why* He controls things the way He does. Why does God allow Satan to be the god of this world? Why is the beast (Antichrist) in the end times allowed to overcome and kill the saints (Revelation 13:7)? Why does God allow suffering in the world?

We live in a world of choices. We step in front of a truck, and we are crushed. We drink poison, and we die. We stand in cold rain with just a t-shirt on, and we get sick. Do we ever wonder why God allows these things to happen?

Cancer, terroristic bombings, and hurricanes bring hurt and harm to those who would otherwise make the choice to avoid risk and harm. It is for these causes of sorrows that many are offended and blame God for lacking compassion. People might be willing to accept the consequences of their choices, but not the consequences for which they had no choice.

Can God prevent suffering and death? Yes, He can, He does, and He will. The question that gets to the point is *why* God does not prevent suffering for everyone right now.

God designed the world perfectly. It is doing exactly what it should be doing. The problem of suffering in creation is the result of sin. The consequences are predictable because of the design of

Suffering and death in a world of sin is no surprise to those who understand the design and the Designer of creation.

creation. The more we learn about the world God created, the better our predictions are. Weather predictions are possible because of our understanding of the conditions that produce weather. The consequences of being exposed to germs, to radiation, and to toxins are predictable. Likewise, the consequences of sin are predictable. Suffering and death in a world of sin is no surprise to those who understand the design and the Designer of creation.

In Romans 8:2, Paul mentions two spiritual laws. "For the law of the Spirit of life in Christ Jesus hath made me free from the law of sin and death." The law of sin and death describes the principle in creation that sin causes death. But the law of the Spirit of life in Christ Jesus can reverse the consequences of the law of sin and death. The law of the Spirit of life in Christ Jesus is the means of obtaining eternal life. These two laws are a part of God's creation, as are the laws of gravity and thermodynamics. They are ubiquitous, and they are unchanging. They make behavior in creation predictable. An action will result in a predictable reaction in accordance to the laws of creation, spiritually as well as physically.

Two important ideas derive from understanding the laws God created to govern the world. First, God is not responsible for the choices others make to sin or for the consequences of sin. He warns us not to sin. We do it anyway. Because we disregard His warnings and laws, we bear responsibility for our

Because we disregard His warnings and laws, we bear responsibility for our choices and the consequences.

choices and the consequences. Second, God designed a perfect world. It is doing exactly what it was designed to do. Left alone without interference or violation of its laws, it would be a perfect place to live. But sin entered the world like a wrench tossed into the gearbox of a machine. The consequences of malfunction were predictable. We now live in an imperfect world.

Cancer is a part of living in an imperfect world. The trillions of cells in our bodies metabolize and multiply every minute we live. Our trillions of DNA molecules are being copied and transcribed trillions of times every minute. Mistakes occur in an imperfect world. I do not blame God for these mistakes. I blame sin. I blame Satan. I blame sinners.

I blame myself for sharing in the sins of this world. I don't blame myself for my cancer, but I share in the blame of making this world imperfect. I find it interesting how people try to shift blame like Adam and Eve did in the garden. Adam blamed Eve, Eve blamed the devil, and in Job 1, we see the devil blaming God. People are so quick to blame God for their miseries. But He deserves no blame. He created a perfect world for us to live in. If there are problems, it is only because we did not listen to Him and follow His instructions.

How does sin produce cancer and disasters? In the beginning, God created—everything. It was a perfect world. Genesis 1 explains the order of creation. Genesis 2 shows us the purpose of creation. God placed Adam and Eve into a beautiful garden. Adam and Eve were in perfect fellowship with God. Every need was taken care of. It was paradise. There was no disease and nothing to be sad about, until they chose to sin. Then fellowship with God was broken. God did not abandon them, but He distanced Himself relationally from them. They chose to be independent, to do their own wills, to sin, and to disobey. So God put them out of the garden to fend for themselves. He would help them as He deemed appropriate, but they chose their own way, so the consequences were theirs to own as well. Because they chose sin, suffering was inevitable. God would no longer protect them and care for them the same way He did in the garden. Paradise was lost because of sin.

The experience of suffering in the world is a predictable consequence of sin in creation. Romans 8:19–22 explains, "For the earnest expectation of the creature waiteth for the manifestation of the sons of God. For the creature was made subject to vanity, not willingly, but by reason of him who hath subjected the same in hope, Because the creature itself also shall be delivered from the bondage of corruption into the glorious liberty of the children of God. For we know that the whole creation groaneth and travaileth in pain together until now." Not only are humans affected by sin, but the physical creation is also affected. The physical creation is corrupted due to the chaos of sin introduced into the world.

The *creature* mentioned in the verse refers to all of creation, animate and inanimate, living and nonliving. God designed a perfect creation, and part of the plan was to subject it to the choices of others. This is the *vanity* being spoken of in the verse. In other words, God created and designed the world we live in to demonstrate the importance of following His instructions. Following His instructions as the Creator and Designer is like following a set of instructions to operate a car. If you don't follow the instructions, the car doesn't run well. Likewise, if you don't follow God's instructions, your life is not as good as it could be.

Can the suffering of the innocent and the suffering caused by natural disasters be due to sin? Yes. These too are predictable in a world of sin. The lesson to learn is that sin does not show favoritism. It is not fair. And it is not merciful. Violence, suffering, cruelty, injustice, and offense are the predictable outcomes of a world polluted with sin. This is not the way God wants the world to be. It is the way the world has become because humanity refuses to heed God's instructions and warnings. Rather than complain about what God is not doing, we should be thanking Him for the grace He has shown to us and complaining about what we are doing. Suffering in the world would be much worse if God was not in control.

We need help. We need a universal reboot. The world is out of our control. And that is the lesson to learn from a world corrupted by sin. We need to return to the Creator. We need to say we are sorry for rejecting Him. We need to ask Him to give us a new start. God is the only one who can make things perfect again.

As for the way things are in the world now, corrupted by sin, we need to endure it until God says it is time to reboot. He has a master plan that encompasses all of creation from eternity past to eternity future. We need to trust God to know best. And it is about time that we do so. Look at the mess we have made in God's creation so far. Obviously, we do not have a better plan. Obviously, we need to hope in God, not in ourselves.

We have every reason to doubt our abilities to make the corrections needed and every reason to believe that God's ways are the best ways. God is worthy of unquestionable trust. He is always in control; He loves us; and He is doing what is best to win the maximum number of souls into heaven. No matter the hardships or atrocities that occur in a world of sin, God is worthy of our trust. This kind of trust is needed for hope and a good prayer life. And remember, if you understand prayer, you will always have hope.

Every crisis is a golden opportunity to honor God in a world of sin and suffering.

Your life circumstances are opportunities to establish common ground with others and to glorify God. When in God's will, there is no crisis that we cannot bear. Every crisis is a golden opportunity to honor God in a world of sin and suffering. Use your life circumstances that way. Rejoice. Don't complain or blame God. Remember, suffering in this world is due to sin. It is the result of choices made contrary to the will, advice, and commands of God. Initially, He gave us a perfect world. We ruined it by refusing to listen to Him. It is time to start listening to Him. Whatever your circumstances, seize the opportunities to be used by God to help others understand that sin is the reason for suffering. Absolute hope for eternal life without sin and suffering is what God offers.

The way you live your life should be a testimony that God deserves to be honored and that believing in Him gives hope. How can you ensure that you don't miss the opportunities to honor Christ? Be saved. Surrender your life to God for guidance. Care about others. Immerse yourself in God's Word, in His Spirit, and in fellowship with others who are doing the same. In time, you will grow spiritually and mature. God's way is the best way to live your life.

GREAT INSIGHTS TO REMEMBER

1. Hope in God is an optimistic expectation without a doubt that God will fulfill His promises.

2. Hope without doubt is based on God's assurance that He will do as He promised.

3. Hope in God begins with believing in Jesus Christ and letting Him save you.

4. Hope removes the despair in a world of suffering and death.

5. Prayers of hope are prayers that come from your heart, not from scripted formulas and repetitive chants.

6. Prayer for the hope of an abundant life makes your life extraordinary.

7. Experiencing God's love and comfort during difficult times reminds us of the future we hope for in Him.

8. Christ's suffering and death were not a defeat. They were the proof of His love for us and the reason we have absolute hope in Him.

9. God's greatest expression of love was His sacrifice to pay for our sins. We do not deserve His love. We are unworthy of His payment. And we certainly do not deserve more.

10. Suffering and death in the world would be worse if God was not in control.

11. Rather than complain about what God has not done, we should be thanking Him for what He has done.

12. God's critics will never be satisfied. They will always find a reason not to believe.

13. Every believer should be a living testimony of hope in God.

GLOSSARY

Accept: To believe; consent as right.

Baptism: Though there are several baptisms such as of the Holy Spirit, of fire, unto Moses in the river, in Christ, etc., most commonly it is thought of as immersion into water as a work of obedience to God in order to qualify for membership in a local church.

Believe: Accepting that God is right.

Believer: One who accepts God's Word as true.

Body: The physical body.

Born again: Born again of God spiritually, thereby having God's righteous nature imputed to one's spirit.

Call: As in Romans 10:13, "For whosoever shall call upon the name of the Lord shall be saved." This means to have the perspective of depending on God.

Carnal: Inclination and perspective of indulging in sinful passions of the physical body rather than delighting in God.

Christ: The second person of the triune godhead known as Jehovah; also known as the anointed One of God, who is God manifested in the flesh (First Timothy 3:16).

Christian: One who is saved by Jesus Christ.

Church: Local assembly of believers who covenant with one another to do God's work God's way.

Communion: Fellowship and close relationship with God.

Confess: As in Romans 10:9, "That if thou shalt confess with thy mouth the Lord Jesus, and shalt believe in thine heart that God hath raised him from the dead, thou shalt be saved." Admission to God that He is right.

Faith: Revelation from God; the substance of things hoped for and evidence of things not seen.

Father: The first person of the triune Godhead known as Jehovah.

Flesh: The physical body, as in carnal.

God: Jehovah; the trinity of Father, Son, and Holy Spirit. Three persons (trinity), yet each being infinitely equal and indistinguishably one in nature, wisdom, power, purpose, and conclusions.

Grace: Favor from God that is undeserved; also referred to as unmerited favor.

Heaven: The dwelling of God where there is no sin.

Holy Spirit: The third person of the triune Godhead known as Jehovah.

Hope: Optimistic expectation especially of the immutable and guaranteed promises of God.

Inward man: The spirit and soul.

Jesus: The second person of the triune Godhead known as Jehovah.

Life: Spiritual life is defined by First John 5:12 as a relationship with Jesus Christ. Eternal life is a never-ending relationship with Jesus Christ.

Lord: A title given to God as the Lord of lords because He is the highest authority in creation.

Mercy: Not requiring that you pay for your crime or receive what you deserve.

Nature: As in the nature of man. It is the innate quality of what you are that determines your tendency and inclination. A sin nature is inclined to do things differently than what God would do. God's nature is the standard of righteousness. (See righteousness and unrighteousness)

New heaven and earth: The replacement creation after the current heaven and earth are melted down and obliterated.

Outward man: The physical body.

Praise: An expression of honor to God.

Prayer because God Answers: Prayer in response to God answering a request.

Prayer because of Revelation: Prayer that is offered because God told one to pray for something.

Prayer for personal desire: Prayer for something one wants.

Prayer for Revelation: Prayer request for God to reveal something such as an idea or guidance for making a decision.

Prayer: Talking to God that involves communion, praises to God, and requests of God.

Repentance: Change of mind and belief.

Request: A question asked of God.

Righteousness: The nature of God that can be given to others through new birth; also known as the born-again experience.

Salvation: God's deliverance of one who believes in Him, His forgiveness of sins, and the miraculous change of one's unrighteous nature to righteousness.

Sanctification: The work of God to make one righteous; the work of a believer to live right for God.

Sin: Anything contrary to God in nature, motive, or deed.

Soul: The conscience and identity of self.

Spirit: The spirit of man which is inseparable from the soul and enables the soul to interact with the spiritual world. (Also, see Holy Spirit)

Spirit-filled: To be under the control and influence of God.

Trust: Rely fully on God; totally dependent on Him.

Unbeliever: One who doubts or rejects God's doctrines and values as being true.

Unrighteousness: The nature of man or angels that is capable of tendencies (motive and behavior) that God would not approve of and is personally incapable of.

Works: Efforts on the part of people to impress God in order to deserve or earn the right to God's blessings. Works are anything a lost person (unbeliever) can do and often involve conforming to the Law of God.

APPENDIX

THE EXERCISE OF PRAYER

- Communion, praise, and requests (CPR) to revive your prayer life
- Minimum requirement for good prayers: faith, belief, righteousness
- The extra mile prayers: persistence and fasting
- Prayer paths with maximum number of souls saved

THE FOUR TYPES OF PRAYER

1. Prayers for revelation
2. Prayers for desire
3. Prayers because of revelation
4. Prayers because God answers

SEVEN MYTHS AND FACTS ABOUT PRAYER

1. God is more likely to answer prayers that are memorized and repeated. FACT: God is not a machine that receives coins to make Him answer prayers.
2. God is more likely to answer prayers that are said in the "best position." FACT: Men of God in the Bible pray

standing, kneeling, and falling on their faces. They lift up their hands, they hold food, and sometimes they do not lift their hands. Some close their eyes. Others do not. Some walk while praying.

3. God does not hear the prayers of the lost nor of the carnal Christian. FACT: God is right next to you. How can He not hear you?

4. God grants all the prayer requests of godly Christians. FACT: Not true. Jesus prayed for the cup of suffering to pass Him. Paul was told no when he asked God to remove the thorn in his flesh. Job was told no for a little while.

5. Prayer should always be offered in the privacy of your personal closet. FACT: Public prayers and private prayers were a part of Israel's and the early churches' experiences. Praying in your closet means praying to God, not to others for their attention, even when offering a prayer in public.

6. Ultimately, prayer is not necessary because God will do what He wants done anyway. FACT: James 4:2 says that you have not because you ask not. If prayer can change things, then failure to pray fails to change things that otherwise could have been changed. Further, God expects you to pray, which means it is necessary to pray.

7. Claim a promise in the name of Jesus, and it will happen. FACT: God only does that which is according to His will, not your will.

ANSWERS TO SEVEN QUESTIONS ABOUT PRAYER

1. Does God need our prayers to make things happen? God does not need our prayers to do His will.

2. Why should we pray if God's will is done without it? God's will is that some things will not be done without prayer.

3. How long should I wait to receive an answer? There is no rule or time table. Only trust and accept whatever the answer is.

4. Is it possible to ask God for something too much? Only if He tells you to stop asking. Otherwise, Jesus said keep asking.

5. If God already knows what we want, why is prayer necessary in the first place? Prayer is not for God. It is for our benefit.

6. Is it okay to ask others to pray for me? Yes. Second Corinthians 1:11 says, "Ye also helping together by prayer for us, that for the gift bestowed upon us by the means of many persons thanks may be given by many on our behalf."

7. What do I do when there are things I do not want to talk to God about? Be honest. He already knows who you are, what you think, what you have done. If you do not want to pray, tell Him. He already knows it. Until admission and confession take place, you will not change.

ONLINE PRAYER COURSE

Go to https://www.patrickbriney.com to continue gaining insights about prayer.

THE AUTHOR

Dr. Patrick Briney is an author, speaker, and Bible teacher for practical Christianity serving as the senior associate pastor at Mission Boulevard Baptist Church in Fayetteville, Arkansas. He is a missionary to the University of Arkansas and is the Founder and President of Leadership Training Institute of America, and the Founder and President of Life Changing Scriptures.

A scientist and former atheist turned Bible believer, Dr. Briney shares from the Bible and from God's designs in creation practical ways to live better, pray better, think better, and lead better.

As a student in 1974 at the University of California at Irvine, Pat was deeply committed to scientific reasoning. In his search to know if God exists, he was confronted with empirical evidence and sound reasons that it was more reasonable scientifically to believe that God did exist than that He did not. He could not deny the possibility of God. God completed Pat's search with personal, divine confirmation by faith. Pat believed and accepted Jesus Christ as his Lord and Savior.

Not long after, the Lord impressed on Pat the importance of

practical, relevant Christianity described in First Corinthians 10:31. He committed everything he did to glorify God, from family to education to ministry. After Pat transferred to the University of Arkansas at Fayetteville, the Lord added him to Mission Boulevard Baptist Church (MBBC) where he continues to teach others the practical, common-sense Christian values, doctrines, and life solutions that make Christianity relevant in today's culture.

While ministering on campus, Pat earned a Ph.D. in microbiology from the University of Arkansas, specializing in immunology and infectious diseases. During that time, he founded the Creation Science Society at the University of Arkansas and produced the Creation Insights seminars. He is regularly invited to conduct seminars on science and faith, as well as creation and evolution, and has debated atheists and evolutionists.

At MBBC, Pat served as outreach director and conducted evangelism campaigns into the community and on college campuses. As the discipleship director, he developed training materials and oversaw the annual MBBC discipleship conference. In 1996, Pat founded the Leadership Training Institute of America (LTIA), where he continues to train leaders to defend and live a Biblical worldview.

Dr. Briney doesn't just talk about being a Christian, he experiences it. When he asked God to teach him about the prayers that move mountains spoken of by Jesus in Mark 11:22–23, God gave him a mountain. Through the experience of stage 4B Hodgkin's lymphoma and its reoccurrence five years later, God granted Dr. Briney's prayer to understand prayer. That was over thirty years ago. He shares his experience and prayer lessons in his two books *HOPE: Lessons from a Cancer Survivor's Journey with God* and *PRAY: How God Answers Every Prayer*.

Pat and his wife, Colleen, live in Fayetteville, Arkansas. They have two grown daughters, a son-in-law, and two very energetic grandsons.

Printed in Great Britain
by Amazon